AMAZING BUT TRUE MORMON STORIES

AMAZING BUT TRUE MORMON STORIES

JOAN OVIATT

Third Printing: March 2005

International Standard Book Number:
0-88290-507-4

Horizon Publishers' Catalog and Order Number:
C1050

Printed and distributed
in the United States of America by

Address:
925 North Main Street
Springville,Utah 84663

Local Phone: (801) 489-4084
Toll Free: 1 (800) SKYBOOK
FAX: (800) 489-1097

Contents

The Gothic Beauty

It had all the elements of a gothic romance novel. Leonora was a young woman of extraordinary beauty, wit and intelligence. Her father was a notorious sea captain who sailed to exotic ports and engaged in nefarious slave trading and—it was rumored—smuggling. The captain was slain in a piratous mutiny.

Leonora's family was left without sustenance, so Leonora set out on her own. She became companion to a wealthy lady, became acquainted with nobility, and soon was invited to live in a castle with the governing family.

At the castle she became best friends with another young woman, Miss Mason. Miss Mason's family was called to serve the new governor of Canada. Miss Mason begged Leonora to go to Canada with her, but Leonora wouldn't leave the land of her birth. Then Leonora had a dream which told her to go, so she accepted the offer of the Mason family and ventured to a new land.

In Canada she attracted the attention of John, a fellow Englishman. John fell in love with Leonora and proposed marriage. She said no. Again she had a dream. In the dream she saw herself happily aligned with John. When John proposed again, Leonora said yes.

This story, though true, would have enough passion and adventure in it to compete with any fictional romance novel. But the story doesn't end there. One day after her marriage, Leonora met a discouraged missionary named Elder Parley P. Pratt who, having failed to convert anybody in Canada, was on his was back to Ohio. Leonora insisted the missionary stop and wait for her husband John to come home. Elder Pratt did as she asked. And that is how the discouraged missionary, who hadn't baptized anyone on his mission, came to meet and convert the future president of the Church, John Taylor, and his beautiful wife, Leonora Cannon Taylor.

Another Mormon Miracle

It was 1837 in Kirtland, Ohio. Joseph Smith was in hiding for his life. Apostate persecutors were seeking him. Numerous lawsuits were filed to bring him into the open, but he couldn't be found, so another target was found—the prophet's father. Father Smith was served with a State's warrant and put in the custody of Luke Johnson, an apostate. Luke knew Father Smith was innocent, and that the suit was instigated by his fellow apostates out of malice. But Luke rather liked Father Smith and didn't entertain the same bitterness that some of his companions did.

When Father Smith was brought to trial, Luke Johnson volunteered to be not only his jailer, but also his legal representative. This delighted the apostate group that Father Smith's defense would be made by a fellow apostate. They couldn't lose, they thought.

The court had an adjoining room that was lighted by one single window. Prisoners could be kept in this adjoining room.

Before the trial, Luke Johnson got access to the adjoining room and "prepared" the window. When the time of the trial came, Johnson told the Judge he would like a few minutes of private conversation with his client. The request was granted and Johnson took Father Smith into the room. When they were both in the room, Johnson went to the window. The window was sealed at the bottom by a nail through the frame. But Johnson had loosened the nail so that it slipped out. He raised the window and helped Father Smith to get out, telling him to go to the nearby Snow house where they would not think to look.

Johnson lowered the window and slipped the nail back into the window frame. He waited a few minutes to give Father Smith time to escape, then he proceeded to the court room where he turned to discover that his client had not followed him. He hurried back to the room to see what was detaining him. He came back into the courtroom looking much disturbed and announced that the prisoner couldn't be found. The men in the court searched the room and the courthouse but Father Smith was gone. The window was discussed as a means of escape but promptly dismissed, for the nail was still in place. The window was still nailed shut.

"How did he make his escape?" was the question on everyone's lips.

The constable, who seemed more astonished than anyone, settled the question by saying, "It is another Mormon miracle."

To Protect a Prophet

Lucy Mack Smith, the prophet's mother, was at home one day when she stepped to the door of her house and looked towards the prairie. A large company of armed men were advancing, but she assumed it was training day and thought nothing of it.

Soon the main body of armed men came to a halt. The officers dismounted and eight of them came into her house. Lucy, thinking they had come for refreshments, offered them chairs but they refused and continued standing. They said, "We do not choose to sit down; we have come here to kill Joe Smith and all the 'Mormons'."

Lucy answered, "What has Joseph Smith done, that you should want to kill him?"

"He has killed seven men in Daviess County," replied an officer, "and we have come to kill him, and all his church."

"He has not been in Daviess County," said Lucy, "consequently the report must be false. Furthermore, if you should see him, you would not want to kill him."

"There is no doubt that the report is perfectly correct," said the officer. "It came straight to us, and I believe it; and we were sent to kill the Prophet and all who believe in him, and I'll be d----d if I don't execute my orders."

"I suppose," said Lucy, "you intend to kill me, with the rest?"

"Yes, we do," returned the officer.

"Very well," said the prophet's mother. "I want you to act the gentleman about it, and do the job quick. Just shoot me down at once, then I shall be at rest; but I should not like to be murdered by inches."

The officer was exasperated. "There it is again," he informed the others. "You tell a 'Mormon' that you will kill him, and they will always tell you, 'That is nothing—if you kill us, we shall be happy.'"

All this time, Joseph had been sitting at a table in the room writing a letter, which he had now completed, so Lucy said, "Gentlemen, suffer me to make you acquainted with Joseph Smith, the Prophet."

The men stared at calm Joseph as if he were a specter. Joseph smiled and, stepping towards them, gave each of them a handshake in a manner which persuaded that he was not a guilty criminal.

Joseph then sat down with the men and explained the views and feelings of the Church. He described the persecution the Church had received from its enemies. He also argued that if any of the members had broken laws, they ought to be tried by law.

The men were expecting to find someone very different than they found. One man said, "This is the last time you will catch me coming to kill Joe Smith or the Mormons either." Another added, "That story about his killing them men is all a lie—there is no doubt of it and we have had all this trouble for nothing; but they will never fool me in this way again; I'll warrant them."

After talking with the men a while, Joseph said, "Mother, I believe I will go home now—Emma will be expecting me." Two men immediately sprang to their feet and declared that Joseph would not go alone, as it was unsafe. They would accompany him to protect him.

And that is how Joseph Smith got a bodyguard escort home, from men who had come to kill him.

The Woman Who Died and Came Back

In 1965 when Dr. Raymond Moody, Jr. was a student, one of his professors related to him the story of how he had died and been brought back to life. The story of what happened to the professor while he was dead amazed Dr. Moody, but because it was a singular experience, he filed it away in his mind.

Years later, when Dr. Moody was teaching at a university himself, a student came to him and related the story of his grandmother who had died during an operation and then had come back to relate her amazing experiences. Dr. Moody was surprised because the story told of events similar to those his professor had related years before.

Dr. Moody began to personally research these near-death accounts. Near-death experiences were not talked about because of social taboos against discussing death and because those few who confessed what they experienced were not believed. Dr. Moody compiled the experiences of one hundred and fifty near-death cases and, in 1975, published his book: *Life After Life.* The intense criticism from much of the scientific community was soon quelled by the thousands of other people who, after publication of the book, came forward to relate their own near-death experiences. People could talk about their experience, because they were not alone. Dr. Moody's research brought the widespread and well-hidden phenomena of near-death experiences out into the open.

A woman named Phoebe once told about her experience with death, she had been overcome with an illness. Her spirit left her body. She saw her body lying on her bed. The women attending her were crying. She saw her husband and her baby near by. While she was watching the scene, two personages entered the room and told her she had the privilege of choosing—she could go, or she could stay with her husband and family. The condition was that if she returned, she must stand by her husband through all the cares and trials he would be called on to endure for the gospel's sake. Phoebe promised the messengers she would do so—she chose to stay with her husband and family.

A spiritual power rested on her husband who, using his priesthood, administered to her body. Phoebe's spirit reentered her body.

Later, she told her husband all she had seen and heard while she had been dead. But it was not Dr. Moody's book that made Phoebe tell her story and caused her husband to record it. The phenomena of near-death experiences was not exposed to the public by Dr. Moody till 1975. Phoebe first died in 1838.

Phoebe held to the promise she made to the messengers. She traveled across a continent and endured the growing pains of a new religion. And for years, till her end, she stood steadfastly by her husband, the prophet Wilford Woodruff.

Christmas In Nauvoo

He was 13 years old, living near Palmyra, New York, when Orrin first heard about a prophet named Joseph who was visited by an angel and given golden plates. Joseph was eight years older than the lad, but Orrin became a constant companion, almost like a little brother to the prophet. Joseph wrote about the lad: "He is an innocent and noble child, and my soul loves him. Let this be recorded forever and ever. Let the blessings of salvation and honor be his portion."

A few years later, in 1843, while on a visit to St. Louis, Orrin was recognized as the prophet's friend by apostates who had him arrested on false charges. Orrin was chained and carried to Independence, Missouri for trial. A grand jury could not find sufficient evidence to bring an indictment against Orrin, but that made no difference to the mob. In spite of his legal innocence Orrin was locked in an underground dungeon for nine months. His wrists were painfully chained to his ankles, even though he was locked up and could be of no harm. The dungeon had a dirt floor with some old straw for a bed. There was no bedding. He had no heat and constantly shivered during the cold months. The dungeon was inhabited by rats. He was fed very little, only scraps, and knew that his captors intended to starve him to death. He lost weight. He was not allowed to shave and the clean-faced youth became disheveled and unkempt.

Sheriff J. H. Reynolds, who held Orrin illegally, wrote to Nauvoo offering to let Orrin go for $5,000 bail, but adding that no Mormons better show up to pay it. At the same time Orrin was offered freedom and money if he would use his friendship to lead Joseph into a mob trap. His answer was, "I'll see you damned first, and then I won't."

In time Orrin was allowed to go to an upper floor of the jail for fresh air and conversation. A family living at the corner of the jail took pity on him and sent him more scraps of food. Mobs often gathered threatening to lynch him.

In fear for his life, Orrin attempted an escape from his illegal imprisonment but he didn't get more than several yards away before a mob surrounded him and he fled back into the jail. Charges were then brought against him for jail-breaking.

Two months later Orrin was brought before a jury in Liberty, Missouri. He was dragged into the courtroom, too weak to stand up by himself. Joseph had managed to raise one hundred dollars to get Orrin legal help. The jury ruled that Orrin's crimes merited a sentence of five minutes in jail.

Even though the jury had legally released Orrin again, his captors would not. They held him for another five hours. At 8 p.m., on December 13, 1843, Orrin's lawyer led him from the jail and told him to run on foot, staying off the main roads, because the mobs would be after him when they learned of his release. In ragged clothes, with no supplies, Orrin ran through the night, hiding in heavy underbrush when mob groups on horseback came by searching for him. He traveled twenty-five miles in one night.

Orrin continued on, heading for Nauvoo, his friends, and safety. Along the way sympathetic people gave him food.

On December 24th, Orrin arrived in Montrose, on the west bank of the Mississippi River. He made the crossing in a small boat. He was now home, but as he walked the streets of Nauvoo, nobody seemed to know him. This once clean-faced, healthy young man now was half his weight, worn and disheveled, and dressed in rags. His face was hardened, as was his spirit, by the long months of imprisonment. The beard that had grown for almost a year was tucked into his shirt, but the long hair went loose down his back, matted and snarled. Friends passed him, but they didn't know him. Orrin decided he would not tell them. He would wait and he would see if anyone recognized him anymore.

It was now Christmas Eve and Orrin made his way to the Mansion House where he hoped to find his friend Joseph Smith. Joseph was there hosting a reception for close friends. Into the middle of their entertainment walked the vagabond, who comported himself in a disorderly manner. Joseph arose and asked the constable to throw the man out. Still not revealing his identity, Orrin continued to act disorderly and refused to leave. Joseph, a champion wrestler, went to assist in the removal. He grabbed the hairy vagabond by the shoulders, then stopped. Looking into his eyes, he recognized his friend.

Tears came to Joseph's eyes and the two men embraced.

It was Christmas Eve, and young Orrin Porter Rockwell was home.

The Disappearing Act of Brigham Young

The place was Nauvoo. The year was 1845. Joseph and Hyrum Smith were dead at the hands of a mob in Carthage. The Mormons were preparing to leave Nauvoo, struggling to sell their properties and to find wagons. Mobs continued to harass the saints. Temple ordinances were being performed at a desperate pace.

One day Brigham Young and several of the Twelve were in the Nauvoo Temple. A marshal and a "posse" of state troops from Springfield had been tipped off as to where Brigham Young could be found. They intended to continue the practice of harassing the saints by arresting them on false, trumped-up charges. This time they planned to arrest Brigham Young on the spurious charge of counterfeiting coins.

The officers arrived at the temple and threatened to search it unless Brigham Young surrendered. Before they could enter, however, George D. Grant, Brigham Young's coachman, brought Brigham's carriage around, and the wiley officers knew that Brigham would attempt to leave. They were waiting for him, however, and Brigham was arrested the moment he stepped out of the temple.

Their prisoners said that he surrendered, but that there must be some mistake; he was not guilty of any such charges. The officers showed him the writ. Though their captive insisted he had a right to call witnesses, the marshal in charge would not wait for any witnesses. He wanted to take the prisoner to Carthage where he'd be "more comfortable." A lawyer, Esquire Edmonds, quickly came along to be the prisoner's legal counsel.

Word of Brigham Young's arrest spread throughout Nauvoo and those on the scene as well as those who came hurrying protested and questioned the officers. Many wept to see their beloved leader taken away.

When the party was safely out of Nauvoo, the officers began to whoop and holler, for they'd finally caught up with the slippery Mr. Young, though their captive again asserted he was not guilty of what was charged in the writ.

In Carthage the prisoner was put in an upper room of the hotel, Hamilton's Tavern. A guard was placed over him. Rumors spread through town that Brigham was in custody and curious people flocked to see him. Brigham was called to dinner where he could be viewed easily by spectators. The officers were more than proud to show off their guest.

Among the visitors was George W. Thatcher, the county commissioner's clerk who was an apostate Mormon. He entered, looked around the room, then asked where Brigham Young was.

"That is Brigham Young," said the landlord, pointing toward the prisoner who was busy eating.

"Where?" replied Thatcher. "I can't see anyone that looks like Brigham."

The landlord told him that it was the fleshy man eating.

Thatcher cursed and said, "That's not Brigham Young; that's William Miller, one of my old neighbors."

The landlord immediately went over and informed the marshal.

The marshal went to Miller and demanded, "Aren't you Brigham Young?"

"No," replied Miller, "I never said I was."

"Why in hell didn't you tell me who you were?" exclaimed the Marshal.

"You did not ask me my name," said Miller.

"Well, what is your name?" said the marshal.

"My name is William Miller."

The marshal turned to Esquire Edmonds, the lawyer who'd accompanied Miller, and asked if the prisoner was Brigham Young. Edmonds laughed and replied certainly not, he'd never said he was. Another witness, William Backenstos, was brought in for identification and swore the prisoner was really William Miller.

The assembled company had a hearty laugh at the officers.

What had happened was that when the officers had arrived at the temple, after getting a tip that's where Brigham Young was, and after a general description, Brigham had had his carriage brought around. He'd given his hat and Heber C. Kimball's cloak to William Miller and sent him down while the ordinances continued in the temple. The people of Nauvoo, hearing their leader was arrested but seeing only William Miller, continued the charade, weeping and protesting.

That night, William Miller remained in Carthage at the home of Jacob B. Backenstos. The next day, when Miller embarked the stage for Nauvoo, one of the marshal's guards threatened his life, but the stage driver told Miller the officers would not be going back to Nauvoo, as, trying to find Brigham Young was like trying to find a needle in a haystack.

William Miller never forgot that night, not only because of the escape of Brigham Young, but because he had spent a sleepless night at the home of Jacob Backenstos. The Lawyer, Esquire Edmonds, also stayed at the home with Miller. Every time Miller tried to sleep he was interrupted by the continued roars of the lawyer's laughter.

The Hidden Ammunition

Nauvoo was in flames. The mobs were laying waste the fields and homes of the saints. Mary, a recently widowed young mother, had made a precarious escape across the river from the city with may of the other saints. But the saints were ill-equipped with little food and few supplies to aid in their survival. Mary made a crucial decision. She must return across the river to Nauvoo to try to save the family cow.

Mary wrapped up her baby, Elizabeth, and left her on the west side of the Mississippi while she crossed back over to Nauvoo. But Mary was too late—the cow was gone. The mob took possession of the river at the crossing, leaving Mary in mob-controlled territory and cutting off her route to safety and to her baby.

Mary stood in this state of terror and desperation when she was approached by one of the mobbers. She admitted to the mobber who she was, told him her name, and told how her baby was on the other side of the river. Somehow her plight touched the mobocrat's heart. He took Mary to the boat that was being used to ferry the guns and ammunition being used against the Saints. He hid her among the guns, and when other mobbers demanded to know what was concealed under the tarp on the boat, the mobber boldly stated, "Nothing but cannons."

Thus Mary was rescued from the midst of the mob by a mobber himself. She was ferried over the river and reunited with her child. The nameless mobber, had, in the midst of hatred and riot, done a noble act. He had also told the truth to his fellow mobber, for the woman he had ferried with the guns and ammunition was a cannon—Mary Edwards Cannon.

The Mystery of the Deserted City

A traveler descending a hillside gazed out upon a city glittering in the fresh morning sun. He saw cool, green gardens and houses for as far as his eye could see. The city seemed to cover several miles, and beyond it were hills checkered with farmland.

He entered the city, but no one was there to meet him. He looked around but saw no one. He could hear no one move. It was so quiet that he could hear flies buzz and water ripple, but there were no human sounds. He walked through the silent streets, feeling that he was in a lonely dream. No grass grew on the paved ways. Footprints were still in the street dust. The traveler continued to walk. He went into empty workshops and smithies. Spinning wheels were stopped. A carpenter had left his shop with shavings still on the floor, and with an unfinished sash and casings still sitting there. Fresh bark was in a tanner's vat. Fresh chopped wood leaned against a baker's oven. A blacksmith's shop had coal heaped for the forge, though the forge was cold. The blacksmith's tools lay nearby, as if expecting their master to return at any time.

The traveler continued to walk. No one stared at him from the windows. He went into a garden, clicking the wicket latch loudly after. He picked some flowers from the garden. He drew himself a drink from a well with a noisy chain. He picked vegetables from the garden. No one came to ask what he was doing. No dog barked in alarm. There was no one.

He thought for a moment that people were hiding in their houses. The doors were unlocked and the windows were open, and when the traveler got the courage to walk into one of the houses, he found it empty. Dead ashes were upon the hearth, still unswept by the housekeeper.

On the outskirts of the town the traveler found the city graveyard, but there was no record of a plague there. There was no difference in this graveyard from others he had seen. Some graves were recent, however, with the mason's ink still visible on the stones. He walked past the graveyard to the fields. An orchard still had fruit. Field upon field of heavy yellow grain lay rotting, unharvested, on the ground.

The man in the empty city was a lawyer. His name was Thomas Kane. Some people had written to him, asking for his help. But those people were no longer in the city, nor was anyone else.

He continued to walk the city, searching. He came to an area where the houses had suffered under cannonade. Then he found mobbers, drunk in a temple, bragging of the people they'd killed.

Thomas understood now. He turned his back on the mobbers and left the city. He left searching for the people who had lived there. He turned his back, just as the citizens had, and sadly walked away from the city of Nauvoo, Illinois.

The Island of Refuge

It was 1846. A ship carrying 235 passengers had rounded the Cape Horn and was heading up the west coast of Chile when it was hit by an unexpected hurricane. The immense waves tossed the ship as if it was made of paper. Waves washed over the decks and into the staterooms. People were lashed to their bunks to keep from being thrown about. One good woman, a mother of seven children, was thrown down a hatchway while carrying a child. She was killed. The passengers were overcome with sickness. The supply of drinking water was almost gone, yet they could make no port. The sails had been taken down; those that weren't were broken. The storm raged on.

Finally, the captain gave up hope. He went to the passengers and told them that in all his years he had never been in a storm such as this, and he knew that the ship could not last much longer. He told the passengers he had done all he could to save the ship, but if they had not made their peace with God, they should do it now as they could go down any minute.

Many of the passengers gathered together, prayed and sang "God Moves in a Mysterious Way" and "How Firm a Foundation." The ship held. Eventually the winds died down. The ship made it into an island harbor. Though the island had been deserted for centuries, there were now three Chilean families living there who could help the people with the ship. The island was a blessing to them for here they renewed their water supplies, caught and dried fish to replenish food supplies, and repaired the ship.

The ship was eventually underway again and the passengers finally arrived at their destination: California.

In 1846, Brigham Young was moving west with the main body of saints. Many members, however, had chosen instead to sail around the Cape Horn to California and travel to the new Zion from there. A group of Mormons chartered the ship *Brooklyn.* Though the captain and crew were not members, the passengers all were. It was this ship, the Brooklyn, that was caught in the tempest and found refuge on an island.

The Mormons were not the only ones who found refuge on this particular island, however. Many years before, a sailor named Alexander Selkirk had been stranded there and managed to survive for several years before being rescued.

A book based on his island experiences was written by the 18th century English author, Daniel DeFoe. Alexander Selkirk was the real-life model for DeFoe's fictional and ever-popular hero, Robinson Crusoe.

A Meeting in California

In 1847 the Mormon Battalion, part of the United States Army, trekked two thousand miles from Fort Leavenworth south into Texas and then up to San Diego in California. From San Diego almost a hundred of them trekked to Santa Ana and then on to Los Angeles.

It was in Los Angeles that Willard G. Smith, a battalion soldier, recorded a strange visit. The company was standing at ease in the street when a dirty, ragged man in ill-fitting clothes came to them. The derelict vagabond accosted Captain Hancock saying, "Gentlemen, I am glad to see you. I have been waiting here days for you, for I heard there was a company of Mormons coming."

Captain Hancock asked the man what he wanted.

The man replied that he had once lived in the state of Missouri. He said, "I hoped there would be some one in the company who had friends killed in the Haun's Mill massacre, who would kill me, because I was there. I was the man who shot that little boy's brains out in the blacksmith shop. His cries and pitiful pleadings have never been from before my eyes and I want to die.

The members of the Battalion knew the story well. A dozen men and two little boys had taken refuge in the blacksmith shop during the Haun's Mill massacre. A Brother Champlain was felled and left for dead, but he had heard the conversations of the mobbers. The two children hid behind the body of their dead father, near the bellows. First one boy was shot and left for dead (though he survived, grievously injured) and the second child, the youngest said, "Please, mister, don't shoot me, I am only a little boy." The mobber replied, "Nits make lice," placed his gun against the boy's ear and fired.

Now that man—the man who had killed an innocent child—stood before the Mormon Battalion. "I shot that boy with a double-barreled shotgun. His pleadings still ring in my ears," the vagabond said to Willard Smith who recorded the event. "I hope you will grant my request." The vagabond fell on his knees saying to Willard, "I want to die; I want you to kill me."

Willard stepped back and said to the man, "There is a just God in Heaven who will avenge that crime. I will not stain my hands with your blood." Then Willard walked away.

The man continued to loiter around the Mormon Battalion camp for days, until officers took him away.

The Haun's Mill massacre occurred on September 6, 1838. Willard G. Smith had been a boy then. He had been at Haun's mill. He had stepped over the body of his dead father to carry out his grievously injured little brother from the blacksmith shop. And he had also carried out the body of his littlest brother. The old vagabond had been at Haun's Mill, but Willard G. Smith had been there too.

The Mystery of the Bad Food

When the Mormon Battalion of the U.S. Army was disbanded in California, many soldiers stayed to find employment, seeking to earn money and purchase provisions before rejoining their families in Utah. One wealthy California landowner hired about fifty of these soldiers.

One day a man came to the employee quarters of the landowner. He was a contractor for the landowner. The contractor announced that some of the workers were needed to build a sawmill for the landowner on the South Fork of the American River. Six Mormon soldiers went with him. They were: Henry Bigler, James Brown, William Johnston, Alexander Stephens, Azariah Smith and William Barger. It is from the journals of some of these men that we have a history of what really happened.

Along with the Mormons and the contractor were four other people: Charles Bennett, William Scott, Peter Wimmer, and Peter's wife, Elizabeth Jane Wimmer. Elizabeth had come along to cook for the men while they built the saw mill. The men did not like Elizabeth's cooking. There was heavy sediment in the water. Elizabeth said the bad meals were not her fault, that the heavy sediment in the water—and gold too—was getting cooked into the meals. The men laughed at her. They were not eating gold! The contractor laughed loudest of all.

On the morning of January 24th, 1848, the men went to the tailrace to see how well the mill was working. Peter Wimmer picked up some bright particles out of the tailrace and noticed how heavy they were. He asked the contractor if he thought they were gold, but the contractor didn't know, so the pebbles were taken to Elizabeth. She tested them in an old kettle and pronounced that they truly were gold. The contractor ordered all the men to be quiet about the discovery. He then took the pebbles to the landowner, who performed a more scientific test. Elizabeth was right. It was gold!

The Mormons wanted to prospect immediately, but they had signed contracts with the landowner. Though they could have broken the contracts and suffered no repercussions, they were men of honor and continued to work for the landowner till their contracted time of service was expired.

Three other men from the Mormon Battalion: Sidney Willis, Wilford Hudson and Levi Fifield were not under obligation. Sworn to secrecy by their brethren, they located a sand bar in the American River that possessed gold. They began operating the mine there and were joined by the other six brethren on March 11, when their contractual obligations were satisfied. Their claim was built up and called "Mormon Island."

In the Congress of the United States, the question of statehood for California seemed an impossibility. Many legislators argued that California was too far from

Washington to be governed. It took a ship sailing around the horn of South America, or a long journey in wagon trains, just to get a message from Washington to California. Other legislators argued that California was mostly worthless land and should be given back to Mexico to prevent a tax burden on U.S. citizens.

The territorial Governor of California was Governor Mason. He and General William T. ("War is Hell") Sherman had other ideas for California. They had heard rumors. Peter Wimmer and the contractor himself had not been discreet individuals. Governor Mason and General Sherman went to Mormon Island to obtain samples from the Mormons. Another Mormon who had joined his brethren, Elder William Glover, helped Governor Mason to pick out the most convincing nuggets.

The nuggets were hidden in an old tea caddy and given to a highly trusted sergeant. The sergeant rode to a port, boarded a ship that sailed for Panama, trudged through the dangerous jungles of the Isthmus of Panama, caught a boat for New Orleans, took a stage to Washington, D.C., and delivered the gold nuggets to President James Polk on December 1st, 1848. On December 5th, President Polk, in possession of the proof that would swiftly guarantee statehood for California, gave his "State of the Nation" speech, mentioning that gold was found in California. This set off one of the greatest gold rushes in the history of the world.

The landowner who hired the Mormons to build his mill, and on whose land the first gold was discovered, was John Sutter. The contractor for the mill was James Marshall. He was given general credit for discovering the gold, though Elizabeth Wimmer argued to the end that she deserved the credit. She had told the men they were eating gold! Though Mormon Island went on record as being the second gold strike, it had the honor of being the first rich diggings discovered in what became known as the California Gold Rush.

The Mormons and the Doomed Wagon Train

On Thursday, April 21, 1846, Brigham Young was in Mt. Pisgah, Iowa. With him was the main body of saints waiting to go West. A lack of supplies, preparation and organization would hold up the main body of saints for a year, but permission was given to a few of the saints to go ahead to the west and explore the territory.

A small wagon train was organized by Brother Thomas Rhoades. With him came his family, including his grown sons and some others. After several weeks of preparations and traveling, they arrived at the Missouri River. They were camped on the Missouri River when two men entered the Mormon camp. The two men were leading a large wagon train, but they were inexperienced and needed a guide. They asked if they might travel along with the Rhoades company. Thomas told them they were welcome as long as they followed the Mormon rules of organization. The men agreed.

Guiding two wagon trains now, Thomas crossed Nebraska to the Platte River. They traveled up the Platte to Fort Bridger. Thomas had his route mapped out. He would travel a well-known explorer's route down through what would become the Salt Lake Valley, and then go across Nevada into California.

Staying at Fort Bridger was a mountain man named Lansford Hastings. He convinced the two men leading the second wagon train that he had found a short-cut to California. He caned the short-cut the "Hasting's Cutoff," claimed that it would save them 600 miles, and sold them some maps he had made. The two men decided to take the short-cut and wanted Rhoades to go with their wagon train. Rhoades warned the men not to take an untried, unknown horse trail with so many wagons and women and children. However, the men chose to believe Hastings the mountain man.

The two companies parted on July 20th. One Mormon woman went with the other company, employed as a washerwoman. Thomas and his company went south, entered California, then traveled up to Sacramento, arriving there in the fall of 1846. Thomas Rhoades met John Sutter, a wealthy landowner who hired the Rhoades family to work for him so that they could renew their supplies.

Thomas inquired at Sutter's Fort about the second wagon train. Nobody had heard of such a group. This was strange to Thomas. The second wagon train was supposed to be traveling 600 less miles and should have arrived in Sacramento before the Rhoades company did. The people around Sutter's Fort assured Thomas that no such wagon train had come through. Thomas looked to the Sierra Nevada mountains with a sense of dread. Often he checked to see if any wagon trains had made it through. None had.

Winter that year came early and hard. Toward the end of January, seven starving people knocked on a remote cabin door. Word was sent from the cabin to the nearby Johnson Ranch. From the Johnson Ranch word was carried to Sutter's Fort: there was a wagon train trapped in the snow in the mountains. Volunteers were called for to rescue the wagon train. Only three men volunteered. Thomas Rhoades heard of the tragedy and went to John Sutter, volunteering his two sons, John and Daniel. He could not go himself for his wife was seriously ill.

John and Daniel Rhoades reached Johnson's Ranch with a few volunteers on February 3, 1847. There weren't enough supplies there to mount a rescue. A volunteer was called for to go back to Sutter's Fort and get supplies. Winter had dealt another blow. The Bear River flooded and the temperatures dipped to sub-zero levels, making the trek back to Sutter's Fort extremely dangerous. But time was of the essence. Only one man volunteered to go back to Sutter's Fort while the freezing river was high. That was big John Rhoades.

John Rhoades returned to Johnson's Ranch with the supplies and an additional number of men willing to be rescuers. Word had spread throughout California about the trapped wagon train and that had brought other donations and volunteers. John guided the volunteers and supplies to Johnson's Ranch.

One of the starving survivors who had made it out of the mountains and to the ranch was Harriet Pike. She knew the Rhoades family. She implored John Rhoades to bring back her two babies. John promised her he would.

John Rhoades and a volunteer named Dan Tucker were the most experienced backwoodsmen and shared most of the responsibility for leading the rescue party.

On February 10th, the rescuers reached a place called Mule Springs. The snow was ten feet deep there. The pack mules they had couldn't make it any further. The rescuers made snowshoes and packed the supplies on their backs.

Many of the volunteers turned back at Mule Springs taking the mules back with them. The rescue effort was too difficult for them.

The remainder of the rescuers continued on, setting fire to dead pine trees to help mark their trail. On February 14th, more men turned back.

Finally, there were only seven men left in the rescue party. Dan Rhoades and Aquilla Glover were worn out, but they refused to stop or go back. They went on. Big John Rhoades continued on also, as did Dan Tucker, Sept. Moultry, Ned Coffeemyer and Joe Sells Foster, each of them pressing their courage and strength to the limit.

The seven men encountered snow as deep as eighteen feet. They dodged avalanches and climbed steep inclines. On February 20th, the rescuers found the camps of the stranded wagon train. There were people John had known. The men chose 23 of the survivors to be taken back, leaving 29 behind to be rescued later. The supplies were soon gone and the rescuers themselves had to ration food for the trip back. John had sought for the children of Harriet Pike. The baby had died but the two-year-old girl, Naomi Pike, was alive. John Rhoades wrapped the emaciated little girl into a blanket which he tied on his back and he carried her all the way back.

Six days journey from the stranded wagon train the seven men and their survivors were met by a second relief party on their way to rescue more of the stranded company.

Dan Rhoades, who made it all the way with the first rescue party, was extremely worn out, and though he lived many years after, he never fully recovered his health. John Rhoades, on the other hand, led a third relief party with a man named John Stark. By the time John Rhoades returned with the third rescued batch of survivors, there were only five people left stranded in the mountains. He begged for enough volunteers to go back for the remainder of the people. Few could be found.

By April 18th, John and Dan Tucker had gathered a few more volunteers and led the fourth and final relief party back into the mountains. When they arrived, only one man was still living. He had become mentally deranged and murdered the other remaining survivors. The rescuers brought the man back with them.

Among the later rescue groups were other Mormons, such as Howard Oakley, from the ship Brooklyn, and First Sergeant Nathaniel V. Jones from the Mormon Battalion. But John Rhoades is remembered best because of his unrelenting courage. Naomi Pike, the two-year-old daughter he carried through the mountains to her mother, lived to be 93 years old. To the end of her life she expressed gratitude to John Rhoades for saving her life and carrying her to safety.

The rescue, of course, is only a part of the tragic story of the Donner-Reed party. The two men who met Thomas Rhoades at the Missouri River to request a guide were George Donner and James Frazier Reed. The so-called "short-cut" pass over the mountains, that the Donner-Reed party died for, is named for them. It is "Donner Pass."

However, this is not the end of the story as far as the Mormons were concerned. Just as Mormons tried to save the Donner party, the Donner party saved Mormon lives. The Donner-Reed party that joined Thomas Rhoades was a large company with substantial wagons. Following trails of explorers, the wagon train blazed a road to the west. It was this wagon road that the Mormons under Brigham Young followed one year later. One part of the road that the

Donner party blazed through the mountains cost them thirty days.

Because of the road, the Mormons went through the same area in four days. George Albert Smith said, "But for the success of the Donner Party blazing a road . . . the Mormon Pioneers might not have reached the Valley early enough to plant potatoes." The LDS Church built the "This is the Place" monument in 1947 to honor the sacrifices of the pioneers. But the Donner party was not forgotten. On the monument was also placed a bronze tablet in grateful remembrance to the Donner-Reed wagon train.

The Non-Mormons Who Saved a Handcart Company

In 1857 Kersten Erickson started west with the seventh handcart company. She was twenty years old, she was thousands of miles from her home in Denmark, she didn't speak English, and she was desperately lonely.

Kersten was assigned to a handcart with only four persons, while most of the others had six people. With her handcart were a sickly girl and an elderly man and wife, so the task of pulling was placed mainly on her. After a while the elderly couple died and she was transferred to a handcart with six pullers, which gave her some relief.

After a month of walking her new shoes wore out. Dead cattle along the trail had to be stripped of rawhide to bind on feet. Nearly all the while the feet of Kersten and others were sore and bleeding. Kersten had no bed covers and had to sleep in an old shawl. The terrain was rough. The days were hot and the nights were sometimes freezing. Food supplies dwindled. Sick, worn out and hungry, Kersten thought of death.

About 200 miles from the end of the journey to Salt Lake City, help came. It was not a Mormon rescue party. It was a group of non-Mormons who came to the aid of the handcart company. The handcart company was allowed to rest while the rescuers fed them. A precious ox was slaughtered and the hungry pioneers had their first fresh meat in days. The kindness of the non-Mormons helped to renew the energies of the handcart Saints, and they pushed on to their destination.

When Kersten arrived, she was so ill and exhausted from her journey that she wasn't expected to live, but with care and kindness she was nursed back to health in her new home in Zion.

Kersten was married to Jens Peter Benson by Brigham Young. When she died in 1910 at the age of 75, she had born nine children, she had 40 grandchildren and three great grandchildren.

Throughout her life, she never forgot the strangers who had treated the handcart company with kindness out on the plains—strangers who had fed them and perhaps saved many lives, including her own.

Kersten never forgot Johnston's Army.

Testimony of Sea Gulls

There are many accounts of how sea gulls saved pioneer crops from the cricket plagues in 1848. The newly planted fields were being devoured by crickets that descended in thick, black clouds on every living thing. The pioneers would have starved if flocks of sea gulls hadn't miraculously filled the sky, then descended upon the pests and devoured them. So go the accounts.

Unfortunately, there were neither supplies nor time to record those on-the-spot testimonies when the sea gull-cricket events occurred. Instead, the accounts were recorded by witnesses in later years. This opened up the door for critics who charged that perhaps the accounts had been embellished to miraculous proportions over those years. Critics have pointed to discrepancies between accounts to show that it might not have happened that way, if it happened at all. After all, critics observed, the sea gull-cricket story is a far-fetched one.

B. H. Roberts, in *A Comprehensive History of the Church,* reflected the testimonies and recollections of those who had been there. He wrote, " (The seagulls) were tireless in their destructive—nay, their saving work. It was noted that when they were glutted with crickets they would go to the streams, drink, vomit, and return again to the slaughter. And so it continued, day after day, until the plague was stayed, and the crops of the pioneers saved."

If anything, the accounts of the birds not only eating the crickets but disgorging them in order to eat more seemed to prove to the critics the exaggeration of the accounts.

In the 1970's, a film company working under the guidance of Hollywood film producer Phil Yordan attempted to portray the life of Brigham Young on film. They needed film of sea gulls devouring crickets.

Steve Cracroft, managing various parts of production including working on the sea gull project, recalls releasing countless crickets to sea gulls, but the sea gulls wouldn't eat them. The sea gulls preferred the anchovy bait that was mixed in with the crickets. This worked for long shots. But they needed close-up film footage of sea gulls devouring crickets.

A number of California sea gulls (the same gull type as from pioneer times) were obtained in San Diego and put in an enclosure with crickets. The sea gulls, however, still proved uncooperative. They wouldn't eat the crickets as long as there was other food available. All other food had to be removed from the enclosure.

Finally, the sea gulls began to eat the crickets and the film crew began filming. Then the film crew noticed something unusual happening. The sea gulls were vomiting up the crickets before eating more. On closer observation it was seen that the gulls didn't vomit up the entire cricket, only the chitinous parts that the birds couldn't digest.

More than a century after the amazing event happened, sea gulls themselves bore witness to the accuracy of those early pioneer accounts. They proved that while the pioneers may not have understood fully the actions of the sea gulls, they told the truth about what they saw.

The State of East California

In 1838, Joseph Smith and companions were held in Liberty Jail. Their suffering there was so severe that it prompted the writing of sections 121, 122 and 123 of the *Doctrine and Covenants.*

The trials the Church leaders endured during this period are well-known events in LDS history. What is not well-known is the great effort exerted by two non-LDS lawyers to save the Mormons. The lawyers were threatened with death by mobs for daring to represent the prisoners of Liberty Jail. They carried their guns with them always, even in court, to protect themselves, and friends continually accompanied them to court to shield them.

The lawyers not only risked their lives but their careers as well, for they defied the commands of the Missouri militia and also Governor Lilburn Boggs, who issued an 'extermination' order. Through the valiant efforts of these two lawyers, the lives of Joseph Smith and his companions were saved, and the Saints went on to accomplish many other things.

In 1850, California was designated a state of the Union. The Utah Territory (also known as "Deseret") had applied for statehood as well, but it was not granted by the Federal

Government—too many people in high places didn't want the Mormons to have the protection of statehood.

When California received its statehood, the people of Utah decided on another plan to be included with the states. Even if the Federal Government wouldn't make Utah a state, there was nothing that said that the state government of California couldn't enlarge its borders to take in unclaimed territory and make Utah part of the state of California. The idea caught fire, and a proposal was sent to California asking to be included in the borders of that state. The proposal indicated that Utah would then be called "East California."

A delegation met with the first governor of the State of California, Governor Peter H. Burnett. Governor Burnett neither hated nor loved Mormons. He was impartial about religion, but he was passionate about Justice. That is why, as a young lawyer, he had laid his life and career on the line to defend Joseph Smith at Liberty Jail. His companion lawyer had been General W. Alexander Doniphan.

The Mormons had brought nothing but problems to Burnett. Still, he believed, justly, that the Mormons were entitled to the rights of U.S. citizens. Governor Burnett took the "East California" proposal and spent much time enlarging and improving it. He submitted the petition to the state legislature. The state Assembly rejected it. The state Senate couldn't come to a conclusion, so they tabled the petition, to be reviewed later.

It has been roughly a century and a half since the California state Senate tabled the petition, and they have yet to consider it.

The Senator Who Stood Against the War

Many speeches have been made on the floor of the U.S. Senate on the subject of war. One such eloquent speech was made by a senator who stood against a war. "Whoever goes there," he said, "will meet the fate of Napoleon's army when he went to Moscow. Just as sure as we are now standing in the Senate these people, if they fight at all, will fight desperately. They are defending their homes. They are fighting to prevent the execution of threats that have been made, which touch their hearths and their families; and depend upon it, they will fight until every man perishes before he surrenders. That is not all. If they do not choose to go into conflict immediately . . . they have provisions for two years; and they will carry on a guerrilla warfare which will be most terrible to the troops you send there. . . . I know not what course will be taken on this subject. I hope it will be one of conciliation. As for the troops . . . fifty thousand would be as inefficient as two or three thousand; and in proportion as you send troops in that vast region, without supplies, and without the hope of them, with no means of subsistence after a certain period, unless it is transported to them, the greater will be your danger. Consider the facilities these people have to cut off your supplies. I say your men will never return, but their bones will whiten [there].

. . . If war begins, the very moment one single drop of blood is drawn, it will be the signal of extermination. Mr. President, in my opinion whether we are to have a war . . . or not, will depend on the fact whether our troops advance; if negotiations be opened; if we understand what (they) are really willing to do; that they are ready to acquiesce in the mandates of the government, and render obedience to the Constitution; if you will take time to ascertain that, and not repudiate all ideas of peace, we may have peace."

This speech was made in the Senate in 1856. The war the senator spoke about was the one President James Buchanan proposed to make upon the Mormons in Utah.

Because of the work of this senator and others, the devastating war that could have been was mainly defused.

The senator who stood in courage in the defense of the Saints had stood in courage both in and out of war. He was experienced with war. He led the armies when Texans revolted against Mexican rule. He was elected the first president of the Republic of Texas, and he later aided the annexation of Texas to the United States. The largest city in Texas is named for him. He was Sam Houston.

Mystery of the Missing Bell

In American towns of the nineteenth century, a town bell in a town meeting house was important to call people together for meetings, to warn them in case of fire or disaster, to celebrate holidays, to toll a birth or marriage or death, and to call the people to worship. A town bell truly was important to a town.

In early Utah the heavy bells needed to serve as town bells were scarce. One bell, however, had been brought across the plains by Johnston's army when it came to put down a "Mormon uprising" that didn't exist. After the army found that no rebellion had occurred, troops were stationed at Fort Douglas to keep an eye on the Mormons anyway. General Patrick Connor had the bell mounted on a cannon carriage and used it to call assemblies.

The soldiers quickly made themselves at home in Salt Lake City (where Fort Douglas was located). They opened up saloons and caroused in the streets, which kept the constables busy. One time a group of loitering soldiers taunted some Mormons with being stupid and incompetent. The Mormons retorted that they could steal the soldier's bell and ceremonial cannon from under their noses if they wanted to. The soldiers laughed and the Mormons went about their business. Over the next days the taunting continued, however, the soldiers daring the Mormons to try their boast.

One dark, rainy night, some Mormon boys decided to show the soldiers. Several of them sneaked into the fort, attached tow ropes to the cannon and bell, hid till the sentry had passed, then pulled the cannon and bell out of the fort. One of the young men sat astride the cannon holding onto the bell clapper to keep the bell silent.

When the soldiers at the fort awoke in the morning, they discovered their bell and cannon were missing. No evidence was left of who the culprits were. Rewards were offered for the bell and cannon. The Mormon boys began to realize how serious their prank was, and they hid the cannon and bell in a barn, covering them with hay.

One day a man named Seth Pixton was up from the southern Utah town of Leeds. He heard about the bell. When he made it known that Leeds was in need of a town bell he was told, "If you'll take the bell to Dixie it is yours." Seth hid the bell in a sack of grain and it was loaded onto his wagon. Nobody could be found to secretly take the cannon, so it was dumped down an old well and buried. But Seth Pixton smuggled the bell down to Leeds where it was used as a town bell in the town church house for many years. The soldiers never did learn what became of their bell or cannon.

Years later, the old bell was replaced in Leeds. It now sits in a museum in Cove Fort, Utah.

The Tale of Two Meals

Sometimes food is the neutral ground that brings enemies together. Two early missionaries were traveling. They had run out of money and food. One day they traveled sixty miles without food. At last they came to a cabin where they stayed the night.

But still, there was no food. As one missionary recorded: "We got up in the morning and walked in the rain twelve miles to the house of a man named Bemon, who was one of the mob from Jackson County. The family were about to sit down to breakfast as we came in. In those days it was the custom of the Missourians to ask you to eat even though they were hostile to you; so he asked us to take breakfast, and we were very glad of the invitation. He knew we were Mormons; and as soon as we began to eat, he began to swear about the Mormons. He had a large platter of bacon and eggs, and plenty of bread on the table, and his swearing did not hinder our eating, for the harder he swore the harder we ate, until we got our stomachs full; then we arose from the table, took our hats, and thanked him for our breakfast. The last we heard of him he was still swearing. I trust the Lord will reward him for our breakfast."

The missionaries who enjoyed such a meal with their enemy were Wilford Woodruff and his companion.

Another meal took place between enemies in Utah in 1854. This time the roles of the Mormon and non-Mormon were reversed. A party of twenty-two men, led by a stout enemy of the Mormons, straggled starving into the settlement of Parowan. They had suffered for days on little food, the previous two days having no food at all. One man in the party had already fallen from his horse, dead of starvation. The same fate awaited the rest of them, had it not been for their coming upon the Mormon settlement. Every family in the Mormon settlement took in one or more of the members of the expedition. They were fed, nurtured back to health, and though the expedition members had no money, the Mormons fitted them out with enough supplies to continue their journey.

Years later the leader of the expedition, whose negative opinions of the Saints were once well-known, was asked to introduce an anti-Mormon lecturer in Los Angeles. The leader answered that he would not associate himself with the lectures because "the Mormons saved me and mine from death by starvation in '54."

The leader of the expedition, whose views were changed by food from his enemies, was John C. Freemont.

The Marvelous Invention

A young English boy named Joseph lived in London. Nearby was a factory. Joseph would often visit the factory, reveling in the mysteries of what was manufactured there and dreaming that one day he could invent such a work.

As Joseph grew, he became a carpenter. In 1851 there was a gold rush in Australia. Joseph took his wife, Adelaide, and their infant son, and they sailed for Australia. Companions on the voyage were a couple named Luke and Christiana Syphus. They were also seeking the gold rush. And they were Latter-day Saints. Joseph and Luke became fast friends. Together Joseph and Luke trekked 400 miles into the Australian bush in search of gold. They found enough for their needs. When they returned from their gold adventures, Joseph was so impressed by Luke that he too became baptized a member of the Church. Joseph moved to Sydney where, in 1853, he bought a two-story house.

Joseph still remembered the dreams of his youth and the factory he had loved. He set about to invent his own creation. It was a rather eccentric thing to do as the invention was large. His neighbors were amazed.

Representatives of the Church in Australia suggested to Joseph that the Church in Utah might need his invention, as they had nothing like it there. Joseph became inspired with the task, developing a conviction that, yes, the Church in Salt Lake City did need his invention and he would do whatever it took to get it there.

In 1856 Joseph and his family sailed on the schooner 'Jenny Lind.' Joseph's invention took up much of the space on the ship. The vessel docked in San Pedro, California. Next, Joseph had to procure wagons to move his invention to Salt Lake City. He was low on funds now and had to stop and work to earn additional funds, but the other Australian saints traveling with Joseph felt the urgency of transporting the marvelous invention and assisted him. Getting the invention to Salt Lake City had become a group effort of the Australian saints.

On June 12, 1857, the invention arrived in Salt Lake City and was given to the Church on behalf of the Australian saints.

The invention was greatly needed and was joyously received. Joseph Ridges carefully and lovingly re-assembled his creation. It had traveled thousands of miles from Australia, and now it was where it belonged. The invention was assembled in the old Tabernacle which was constructed of adobe.

The Church had a choir, the forerunner of the Mormon Tabernacle Choir, but they had had no organ—till the Australian saints brought one half way across the world over mountains, deserts and seas.

In 1863, when the new Tabernacle was being constructed, Joseph Ridges was called by Brigham Young to oversee arrangements for the building of a new organ for that building. Parts of the Australian organ stayed in the Assembly Hall for many years. And that is the history of the first Tabernacle Organ.

The Settlement that Failed

When Brigham Young established Salt Lake City, he also established scores of other settlements across the West. The settlements were up in Idaho, down in Arizona, all over Utah, across Nevada, even in California. The settlements touched on other states as well. Many of these settlements survive as cities today. However, some of the settlements failed.

One such settlement seemed to have great promise. The location was chosen because it was an oasis on the old Spanish Trail. John C. Freemont and Jefferson Hunt had seen the oasis on their explorations. Though there had never been a settlement at the oasis before, the many springs promised that crops could be grown. Brigham Young called members to go to the oasis and build a settlement there in 1855.

Within months of arriving at the oasis, streets and fields had been surveyed. Corn, wheat, squash, melons and a number of vegetables were growing. Oats, cotton, beans, and grapes were soon added, aided by irrigation. Timber was hauled from the mountains. A fort, 150-feet square with walls reaching 14-feet high, was constructed. Houses and storage buildings were erected over the years. A post office was established there. A lode of lead ore was discovered nearby and a mining company was begun. The community boasted a choir and a weekly lyceum. Missionaries were sent to preach to nearby Indian groups. Wagon trains stopped at the settlement, thus making it a trading post as well.

In spite of all its promise, by 1857 the settlement was failing. The farmers disliked the heat. The mine failed. The Indian mission was a failure. Range vegetation was too sparse to support growing herds. Many feared Johnston's army that was moving toward Utah. At last Brigham Young officially ended the "callings" to the oasis settlement and most settlers chose to leave. In 1858, only five men remained. Though still used as a stopping place for travelers, the settlement was primarily a ghost town.

Had the mine not failed, the settlement might have continued. Lead and iron were badly needed in the territory, but the lead that was produced from the ore was too flaky and brittle. It was not till later, after the mine was abandoned, that California miners learned why the lead from the Potosi mine was brittle, and benefitted from that knowledge. It seems that the lead had a much-too-high content of zinc and silver. Though the Mormons abandoned the mine, they still had a right to be proud of the first lode mining in the modern history of the territory that would become Nevada.

As for the settlement, many say it didn't really fail, it was just postponed for a while. What else can be said of a city that now boasts over 60,000 Latter-day Saints, who comprise over 12% of the population; that has 16 stakes of the Church in the area, that even had its own temple dedicated in 1989.

A huge city has since grown out of the little Mormon settlement on the oasis called "Las Vegas."

The Chicken that Prophesied

In the 1860's, when Paris, Idaho was still a young settlement, a remarkable thing occurred. A woman by the name of Clifton owned a Plymouth Rock hen which laid large, distinctively brown eggs. One day a neighbor, Joseph, dunked one of the eggs into water. He was astounded to see an inspiring message appear. He took his discovery to the other neighbors. Another egg was obtained. Joseph followed the same procedure. Before the eyes of witnesses a message appeared on that egg.

For awhile, Joseph continued to get eggs from Mrs. Clifton's chicken. Before gatherings of people, he'd dip the eggs in the water and out would come messages of inspiration, scriptural passages, and spiritual advice. Soon the eggs started prophesying the future.

Speculation and excitement ran high. Most people probably didn't believe in it, even though they saw it, but credulous people took the messages to heart.

Word finally reached Salt Lake City and Apostle Charles C. Rich of the Council of Twelve was dispensed to look into the matter.

On arriving in Idaho, Elder Rich went directly to the young man who was furnishing the "water" into which the egg was dipped. He knew this young man knew about chemistry. He went to this young man because he had access to the poor woman's hens. He went to this young man because he knew that whatever was going on had to do with this particular young man, because this young man was his son, Joseph C. Rich.

Joseph had been writing on the eggs with invisible ink, which was brought out when exposed to the fluid he furnished. Speaking at a public gathering, Apostle Rich assured the people that if the Lord wanted to reveal His truths to the people, He would do so through his recognized authority, and not through the "hind end of a hen."

On One Day

The date of April 6 is an important date to Latter-day Saints. On that day in 1830 The Church of Jesus Christ of Latter-day Saints was first organized.

April 6th is an important day in modern times for other reasons as well. On April 6, in 1789, the first Catholic Diocese was founded in the United States—in Baltimore.

On that same day the United States Senate and House of Representatives, in its constitutional form, assembled together for the first time.

On April 6, 1840, Brigham Young, Heber C. Kimball, Parley P. Pratt, Orson Pratt, George A. Smith and Reuben Hedlock landed in Liverpool, England, to take the gospel abroad.

On that same day in Nauvoo it was announced that the time had come for the gathering of the Jews and that Jerusalem would soon be rededicated.

On April 6, 1841, the first stone was laid for the Nauvoo Temple.

On that same day John Tyler was sworn in as the 10th President of the United States, following the death of President William Henry Harrison.

On April 6, 1896, the first modern Olympics were held in Greece.

On April 6, 1909, Robert Edwin Peary became the first man in written history to reach the North Pole.

On April 6, 1917, President Woodrow Wilson and the United States Congress issued a declaration of war. The U.S. was now part of the "War to End All Wars," World War I.

There were other wars on April days when men were dying while nature was being reborn. In 1832 Joseph Smith prophesied the Civil War would occur (*Doctrine and Covenants,* section 87). Thirty years after that prophecy, Union and Confederate troops gathered at a small, log church to engage in the largest battle in United States history up to that time. The church, whose name meant 'peaceable,' was better know as 'Shiloh.'

On that same day the Confederate commander lost his life on that battlefield, not far from the church. The commander of the Confederate forces had more in common with the Latter-day Saints than a prophecy. A few years before he had led an army to Utah to put down a rumored rebellion that didn't exist. The army he led then is still known in American history as "Johnston's army," after General Albert Sidney Johnston, who died at Shiloh on April 6, 1862.

The Grave with Nobody in It

In the Salt Lake City cemetery there is a grave with nobody in it, or, more appropriately, no *body* in it. How this came to be is associated with perhaps the strangest speech ever given in the Salt Lake Tabernacle.

In 1862 a young outlaw named Moroni Clawson was gunned down in Salt Lake City in a shootout with police officers. Because young Clawson had no means, city police officer Henry Heath paid for burial clothes for him. A week after the burial on January 27, 1862, Clawson's brother, George Clawson, came to remove the body to Willow Creek (now Draper, Utah). When George opened the coffin, he found his brother's body stripped of clothing and accused the city of burying his brother in disgrace. Officer Heath denied the charge, having personally seen to the burial himself. An investigation was commenced. The investigation ended at the home of the city grave-digger, Jean Baptiste—a wormy, private man who seldom talked though he'd worked for the city about five years.

Baptiste was not home, but his feeble-minded wife was. As the officers tried to question her, they noticed a large box, which upon investigation, they found was filled with burial clothes. Other boxes were opened. They were filled with all manner of men's, women's and children's clothing, shoes and jewelry. Some planks of coffin wood were found stacked for use as fire wood.

Jean Baptiste was located at the cemetery, where, when confronted by the officers with the evidence, he confessed to robbing about a dozen graves. He could not explain about sixty pairs of children's shoes and clothes, plus numerous other articles of men's clothing and women's suits and dresses.

Later estimates were given that Baptiste had robbed as many as 300 graves. Hundred of people turned up at the Court House to examine the clothing and possibly identify some of it as belonging to a loved one. Officer Heath remembered mothers sobbing when identifying the burial clothes of a child.

All of Salt Lake City was shocked and outraged. There was talk of hanging Jean Baptiste. Mobs formed nightly at the jail. The legal system was at a loss about what to do with him because there were no penalties on the books that dealt with this kind of crime.

Finally it was decided that the grave robber would be banished to Freemont Island out on the Great Salt Lake. Six weeks later on a regular visit to check up on him, officers found that Jean Baptiste had escaped. Planks of wood from his hut were gone, as was the hide of a cow, leading officers to believe he had made a raft.

Jean Baptiste was never recaptured, and for years afterwards Utah children had their own version of the 'boogie man.' Lurking out there, somewhere, in the dark.

Meanwhile, many of the citizens of Salt Lake City were troubled that their loved ones would be resurrected without any clothes on. This prompted Brigham Young to give one of the strangest discourses of his career, on whether it was necessary to dig up deceased persons to dress them again. He said that he had several loved ones buried in the city cemetery and said he would not open their graves, for, he said, "I will defy any thief there is on the earth or in hell to rob a Saint of one blessing." However, he advised others to "Pursue the course that will give you the most contentment and satisfaction," though he promised that the resurrected saints would not have to worry about earthly clothing, for they would come forth beautified and clothed with glory.

Several graves were reopened. Much of the burial clothing was reclaimed. But the remainder of the clothing was gathered together and buried in a single grave in the cemetery. There are no dead in that grave, only their clothing.

News Report on the Amazon

On June 4, 1863, a news reporter wrote a story from an English dock. "I go aboard my emigrant ship," he wrote. "Nobody is in ill temper, nobody is the worse for drink, nobody swears an oath or uses a coarse word, nobody appears depressed, nobody is weeping, and down upon the deck in every corner where it is possible to find a few spare feet to kneel, crouch, or lie in, people, in every unsuitable attitude for writing, are writing letters.

"Now, I have seen emigrant ships before this day in June. And these people are so strikingly different from all other people in like circumstances whom I have ever seen, that I wonder aloud, 'What would a stranger suppose these emigrants to be!'

"The vigilant bright face of the weather-browned captain of the *Amazon* is at my shoulder, and he says, 'What indeed! The most of these came aboard yesterday evening. They came from various parts of England in small parties that had never seen one another before. Yet they had not been a couple of hours on board when they established their own police, made their own regulations, and set their own watches at all the hatchways. Before nine o'clock the ship was as orderly and as quiet as a man-of-war. . . . A stranger would be puzzled to guess the right name for the people. . . ." The captain went on to say, "If you hadn't known, could you ever have supposed?"

"How could I!" answered the reporter. "I should have said they were in their degree, the pick and flower of England." Then the reporter went on to ask how many were on the ship.

"Eight hundred in round numbers . . ." answered the captain.

"Eight hundred Mormons." the reporter exclaimed. He then continued to write: "I . . . had come aboard this emigrant ship to see what eight hundred Latter-day Saints were like. and I found them (to the rout and overthrow of all my expectations) like what I now describe with scrupulous exactness.

The reporter went on to interview the Mormon agent and others on the ship. He finished his report on the Mormons by writing, "I afterwards learned that a dispatch was sent home by the captain before he struck out into the wide Atlantic, highly extolling the behavior of these emigrants, and the perfect order and propriety of all their social arrangements. What is in store for the poor people on the shore of the Great Salt Lake, what happy delusions they are laboring under now, on what miserable blindness their eyes may be open then, I do not pretend to say. But I went on board their ship to bear testimony against them if they deserved it, as I fully believed they would; to my great astonishment they did not deserved it; and my predispositions and tendencies must not affect men as an honest witness. I went over the Amazon's side, feeling it impossible to deny that, so far, some remarkable influence had produced a remarkable result, which better known influences have often missed."

The reporter's heart was changed. His report, unfortunately, changed few other hearts and was forgotten over the years. Some of the reporter's other writings were not forgotten, however. His *Oliver Twist, David Copperfield,* and *A Christmas Carol,* became catalysts for social and moral change. The reporter was Charles Dickens.

The Trousers that Shocked Utah

In the 1930's and 1940's, Katherine Hepburn popularized women's trousers on the silver screen. Prior to that, wearing trousers had never been a fully accepted fashion for American women. Yet, as early as the 1860's, an attempt had been made to put trousers on a female population—and it happened in Utah.

Salt Lake City was still a growing western town, with dirt streets and few sidewalks. It was often difficult for a woman in skirts to navigate her way through the muddy streets of the city. Work in the fields was even more encumbered by the heavy skirts.

It was then that a Utah gentleman was struck with an idea. Why not follow the example of men, and put women in trousers?

The man, aided and abetted by his wife, Eliza, set about to make his idea a reality. He would design the perfect female outfit. It would, above all, be modest. And it would be simple—no frills or such nonsense. It would be practical, utilizing less material than the contemporary dresses with all their excess yardage. And it could be mass produced, for all women could use the same design.

The design was finally finished. It included a cape for cool weather, and a beaver hat (not a bonnet) to protect delicate heads from the elements. The main part of the outfit was a high-necked, long-sleeved, buttoned-in-the-front, plain dark dress that reached shockingly only to mid calf. And under the dress, protecting female modesty, were the trousers.

The designer and his wife triumphantly showed his design to the other women in his family. But, instead of a warm reception, the women in his family were dismayed and appalled. They would sacrifice and go anywhere for him; move to the most desolate settlements of the territory for him; they would give up comfort and possessions for him. But they would *not* wear that outfit!

The outfit became a widespread subject of discussion in the community. Some acknowledged the practicality. Others laughed at the absurdity of such a radical fashion. Some ladies made their own prophecies that women would "never wear trousers.

The idea, later called the "Deseret Dress," was a complete failure. And that's why Brigham Young gave up designing women's fashions.

Mouth-to-Mouth Resuscitation

Four missionaries were traveling by boat in Hawaii. As they attempted to make harbor, violent waves pushed the boat onto a coral reef, capsizing the boat. The people on the island shore, seeing the accident, manned lifeboats and hurried to the aid of the crew and passengers of the boat. Three of the missionaries made it into a lifeboat, while the rescuers frantically searched for the missing missionary. One of the rescuers finally located the fourth missionary under the water when his body touched the rescuer's feet. The drowned missionary was dragged into the lifeboat where his body lay lifeless.

Two of the missionaries immediately administered to the drowned missionary. The rescuers soon had the missionaries on shore where the drowned missionary was rolled and pressed to get the water out of his lungs. The missionaries and the crowd labored on the drowned one for some time. but there was no sign of life.

Eventually, bystanders said there was nothing more that could be done, but the other missionaries wouldn't give up. They continued to work over him and to pray that the lord would spare the missionary's life so that he might return to his family. They prayed and listened for the Spirit to tell them what to do.

One of the missionaries, Elder Cluff, later related what happened. "Finally, we were impressed to place our mouth over his, and make an effort to inflate his lungs, alternately blowing in and drawing out the air, imitating, as far as possible the natural process of breathing. This we persevered in until we succeeded in inflating his lungs. After a little, we perceived very faint indications of returning life. A slight wink of the eye, which until then, had been open and deathlike, and a faint rattle in the throat, were the first symptoms of returning vitality. These grew more and more distinct, until consciousness was fully restored."

The drowned missionary, upon awakening, inquired as to the welfare of his companions and was assured that they were all right.

Thousands upon thousands of lives have been saved by the mouth-to-mouth method of artificial respiration since it was first advocated by the American National Red Cross and the American Medical Association in the early 1960s. What is unusual about this incident is that it occurred in 1864, long before the concept of mouth-to-mouth resuscitation was developed. The action performed by the missionaries amazed onlookers as well as themselves. Yet, through the Spirit, the missionaries knew it was the thing to do.

What else was unusual about the incident was that the drowned missionary who was brought back to life was Lorenzo Snow. He later became the fifth president of The Church of Jesus Christ of Latter-day Saints.

The Missionary Who Would Be King

Missionaries have been known to get themselves into trouble while on their missions. But probably none have gotten themselves into as much trouble as Elder Walter Murray Gibson.

The early missionaries in the Hawaiian Islands enjoyed success. There were over three thousand members there when the missionaries were called back to Utah in 1857 because of the "Utah War." The Hawaiian saints were left without central Church leadership.

In 1861, Elder Gibson arrived in Hawaii. He was sent as a regular missionary by Brigham Young, but Elder Gibson told the Hawaiian saints otherwise. At the 1861 October conference in Hawaii, Gibson told the members that he had been sent to be in charge of the Church in Hawaii. He called himself "Chief President of the Islands of the Sea and of the Hawaiian Islands, for The Church of the Latter-Day Saints."

Among his first official acts he sold certificates of membership to those who wished to remain active. Any who wished to retain or gain the honors of priesthood positions had to pay for them. Many people paid dearly. Gibson sold positions of bishops, seventies, apostles, first presidencies and even the position of archbishop to those who could afford it.

All the while Elder Gibson kept writing to Brigham Young, telling how well his mission was going—withholding from President Young the accounts of what he was really doing.

Finally Elder Gibson convinced the members that to truly do the work of the Lord, they must give him all the money and livestock they possessed. They must also sign over their land deeds to him. A gathering place would be established on the island of Lanai, and centered in the Valley of Palawai. All the members were to gather to Lanai where Elder Gibson would assign them to farming and to building a city for him. In return, the members would be given food once a day. In his journal Elder Gibson wrote:

"I could make a glorious little kingdom out of this, or any such chance, with such people; so loving and obedient.. . . I would fill this lovely crater with corn and wine and oil and babies and love and health and brotherly rejoicing and sisters' kisses and the memory of me for evermore."

Gibson commanded that all the Church lands and chapels on the other islands be sold and the money given to him. For two-and-a-half years faithful members strove to satisfy "President" Gibson. Gibson spoke condescendingly to and of the members for their faith. He wrote in his journal, "I view him (the Hawaiian) and treat him as an interesting yet feeble younger brother, a subject of an oceanic empire. . . . Who or what shall I fear where I am King.. . . . I am King; not of oceanica, not of Malaysia, not of Hawaii nil, not of Lanai, but of Palawai on this day of grace. But this is but the baby of my Kingdom. Oh smiling Palawai, thou infant hope of my glorious kingdom."

What Gibson didn't know was that the natives were not so simple. They had put their faith in him in the beginning, but many questioned why Gibson's policies were contrary to what they had learned from the missionaries in the beginning. Unbeknownst to Gibson, some members wrote letters to church headquarters telling what was really happening.

Mail was slow in those days. It had to cross the Pacific Ocean, then go by wagon train from California to Utah. Transportation was just as slow, which explains how Elder Gibson got away with what he did for two-and-a-half years. When five missionaries sent by Brigham Young showed up on his doorstep, Elder Gibson looked more surprised than glad.

It took several months for the missionaries to straighten out the mess that Elder Gibson had made of the Church in Hawaii. All Church funds and lands were now in Gibson's name and he refused to give them back to the Church or to the members whom he had defrauded. The Church did not care for litigation and felt the welfare of the people to be the primary concern, so instead of fighting in court, they worked to dismantle Gibson's "kingdom" and return the Hawaiian saints to the other islands and to more normal lives. The saints, however, had the option of staying in Gibson's "kingdom" if they wanted to, but they all left except for fourteen of them. Walter Gibson was then king over only fourteen people. This did not suit the man who longed to be a big king.

Walter Gibson was disassociated from the Church. But he put his talents and new wealth to other use—becoming friendly with the royalty of the Kingdom of Hawaii. No, they did not make him king of all Hawaii, but he got the next best thing. He was made prime minister of the Hawaiian kingdom, in which position he served from 1882 to 1887.

The City of Wealth

In July of 1847 the saints came to the Salt Lake Valley. Exploring parties searched the surrounding areas. One party climbed to a summit of the Wasatch Range, where they looked down into a wealth of lush, forested valleys. Parley P. Pratt was a member of this expedition. In his honor, the place was named "Parley's Park."

Within half a dozen years, the land of Parley's Park was deeded to various settlers for timber work or agriculture.

In 1862, Colonel Patrick Edward Connor, a non-Mormon, established headquarters at Fort Douglas in Salt Lake City. He was a man after wealth, and he encouraged his troops to spend their time prospecting. Feeling outnumbered by the Mormons, he also encouraged outside settlers to come into the area by claiming there were precious metals to be found.

By 1870, 164 mining claims were filed in Parley's Park, mostly for silver and lead. In 1872, the rich Ontario Mine was discovered.

A Mormon by the name of George Snyder lived in Parley's Park. He opened a sawmill and began building for the influx of miners coming into the area. A boom town began to take form. There was no name for the town, though some referred to it as "Upper Kimball's" or "Upper Parley's." Brother George Snyder decided to name it. He even ran up a flag with the town name on it.

Today the rich mining operations are gone. Instead, the town derives its wealth from snow. It is now a world renowned ski resort. Parley's Park City became known, simply, as Park City.

The Mule that Saved the Mexican Saints

Lot Smith, an early frontiersman and captain in the Union Army, had a reputation as a tough, rugged and undefeatable pioneer who had even outdone Buffalo Bill Cody in horsemanship. Yet—as with all tough reputations—Lot was often expected to defend it.

One day a man by the name of Sol Hale, a strapping giant, came up to Lot Smith and said, "I'll bet you $5.00 I can throw you in the river, Captain. But you've got to give me three trials."

Captain Smith looked over this large man and answered, "Soloman Hale, do you suppose I want to get thrown in the river three times?"

Eventually Lot Smith went down to Mexico to help the Mormon colonies down there. But, as everywhere, people arose who didn't want Mormons in their midst. One day a large mob came and surrounded the colony, ready with their weapons to annihilate the Mormons. Under the pretext of giving the colonists a fair chance to save their lives, the mob leaders made a proposition. If any of the Mormons could ride one of their wild Mexican mules, they would spare the lives of the Mormons. The mule that the mob leaders had picked out was said to be so wild that no one had ever ridden him.

The mob leaders taunted, daring anyone to volunteer. Lot Smith came forward.

One of the men asked, "Are you the one who is going to try riding this mule?"

Lot Smith answered, "No, I'm not going to *try,* I'm going to *ride* him."

Lot got on the mule and the mule lived up to his reputation. He bucked, spun, pitched, and tried every trick to throw his rider. But Lot Smith lived up to his reputation as well. He stuck to the mule like fly paper. The mule, in a panic, took off running.

Lot Smith had a long, flowing red beard. When the mule streaked past the people with Lot's red beard "parted in the breeze and streaming out behind him on each side of his face," it was said that he looked like streaks of red flames in the sunset. It was an amazing sight. The mob relented.

And that was how Lot Smith and the mule saved the lives of the Mormon colonists in Mexico.

Among the Awful Mormons

A young man named Sam wanted a job. As his older brother had been appointed a territorial secretary in Nevada, Sam decided to accompany him west and try to also get a job in Nevada.

One of the highlights of his trip west was Sam's stop in Salt Lake City. As Sam wrote, "We walked about the streets . . . and there was fascination in surreptitiously staring at every creature we took to be a Mormon. This was . . . a land of enchantment, and goblins, and awful mystery. We felt a curiosity . . . and we experienced a thrill every time a dwelling-house door opened and shut as we passed, disclosing a glimpse of human heads and backs and shoulders—for we so longed to have a good satisfying look at a Mormon family in all its comprehensive ampleness, disposed in the customary concentric rings of its home circle."

Sam went on to record, "The second day, we made the acquaintance of Mr. Street . . . and went and paid a state visit to the king (Brigham Young). He seemed a quiet, kindly, easy-mannered, dignified, self-possessed old gentleman of fifty-five or sixty, and had a gentle craft in his eye that probably belonged there. He was very simply dressed and was just taking off a straw hat as we entered. He talked about Utah, and the Indians, and Nevada, and general American matters and questions, with our secretary and certain government officials who came with us. But he never paid any attention to me, notwithstanding I made several attempts to "draw him out on federal politics and his high handed attitude toward Congress. I thought some of the things I said were rather fine. But he merely looked around at me, at distant intervals, something as I have seen a benignant old cat look around to see which kitten was meddling with her tail. By and by I subsided into an indignant silence, and so sat until the end, hot and flushed, and execrating him in my heart for an ignorant savage. But he was calm. His conversation with those gentlemen flowed on as sweetly and peacefully and musically as any summer brook. When the audience was ended and we were retiring from the presence, he put his hand on my head, beamed down on me in an admiring way and said to my brother: 'Ah—your child, I presume? Boy, or girl?'"

Young Sam had many criticisms of his stay in Utah, as well as compliments. For example, he wrote: "Salt Lake City was healthy—an extremely healthy city. They declared there was only one physician in the place and he was arrested every week regularly and held to answer under the vagrant act for having 'no visible means of support.'"

Eventually Sam went on to Nevada where he was a reporter for the *Territorial Enterprise.* He published an account of his trip through Utah, in 1872. Titled *Roughing It,* Samuel Clemens published the book under his pen name—Mark Twain.

The Pants Rebellion

The community of Orderville was founded in early Utah by Saints attempting to live the law of consecration. All goods were held in common. The community was run by committees. Any profits from the community businesses were turned over to the Perpetual Emigration Fund to help other pioneers make their way to Utah. In this way, the community of Orderville assisted hundreds of pioneers over the years in making their journey to Utah.

It was not easy living in a communal society, however. One young man decided he needed new trousers. Young people in other communities had newer clothes than did the youth of Orderville. The young man went to the clothing committee and applied for a new pair of trousers. But there were no holes in his trousers, and there were no patches, so the committee turned him down.

The young man then set about devising a plan to get himself some new-fashioned trousers. When herders docked a large herd of lambs, the young man went to the sheep sheds, gathered up the tails and secretly sheared them himself. When the shipment of wool was sent to the town of Nephi, the young man went along, carrying his own small bag of wool, which he exchanged for new store-bought trousers.

When the young man returned to Orderville, his new trousers created a sensation. The young man was brought before the Board of Management where he was commended for his ingenuity. But, because it was a communal society he was told that he would have to give up the pants, as all Orderville men were to wear the same cut and material of trousers. However, to make it up to the young man, they would take the pair of pants, unseam it, and use it as a pattern for all the trousers to be made for the community—and he would get the first pair.

In the following weeks the sewing department was swamped with orders for new trousers. The trousers, especially of the boys, suddenly were wearing out at an alarming rate, and there seemed to be a coincidence in the way that the pants were worn out. Instead of wearing out at the knees or cuffs, the pants were all wearing out at the seat. Some of the elders began watching the boys to see what was making the pants wear out so fast. The boys were finally followed into a shed where the grindstone was kept. There the secret was uncovered. While one boy would bend over, his behind pressed against the grindstone, another boy would turn the grindstone, grinding off the seat of his pants.

The elders of the community saw the humor of the situation and sent off a load of wool to be traded for cloth. Now all the young men in Orderville could have their own pair of new-fashioned trousers.

Ever after that the incident was referred to as "The Pants Rebellion "

A Road By Any Other Name . . .

The Transcontinental Railroad was finished in 1869, but the Union Pacific continued to expand its tracks across the territory. As the Union Pacific expanded, men willingly left their fields to work on the railroad, and women would leave their duties to prepare meals for the workmen. The pioneers cooperated when something big needed to be accomplished. Pay from the Union Pacific railroad was uncertain. In the end the Union Pacific owed six hundred thousand dollars in debts to the local contractors.

Brigham Young and the contractors negotiated and received instead six hundred thousand dollars' worth of rails, locomotives, cars, etc., which were eventually used in building up the locally owned Utah Central Railroad.

The right-of-way for the Utah Central Railroad was usually granted by the settlers readily. The railroad was necessary for economic growth. However, a man by the name of Wood had been on a mission and when he came home he found the railroad running right in front of his house. Because he had been on a mission, no one had asked his permission. Brigham Young was pushing the railroad to go through as soon as possible, so it was built without Elder Wood's permission. Elder Wood went to see Brigham Young and angrily accused him of usurping authority to build a railroad right past his front porch. Brigham Young's first response was to ask Brother Wood about his mission. Brother Wood was so angry he wouldn't tell President Young anything about it. Then Brigham Young said, "All right, we have been hunting for a name for this little place and now we have one. We'll call it Woods Cross."

The town of Woods Cross, Utah, is still thriving today.

A Sermon About Nothing

The young missionary was serving in Jeffersonville, Virginia. The lawyers and ministers in the vicinity were amazed he could deliver such powerful sermons without much preparation. Some of the men offered to arrange a meeting for him if he would agree to speak on any subject they desired. However, he would not know his topic till he arrived at the meeting.

The missionary saw an opportunity and agreed. The meeting was arranged. When he arrived, the missionary went to the pulpit where he was handed a piece of paper containing his topic. He opened the page. It was blank. The following is a record of his discourse:

"My friends, I am here today according to agreement, to preach from such a text as these gentlemen might select for me. I have it here in my hand. I don't wish you to become offended at me, for I am under promise to preach from the text selected; and if any one is to blame, you must blame those who selected it. I knew nothing of what text they would choose, but of all texts this is my favorite one.

"You see the paper is blank." He held up the paper. "You sectarians down there believe that out of nothing God created all things, and now you wish me to create a sermon from nothing, for this paper is blank.

"Now, you sectarians believe in a God that has neither body, parts nor passions. Such a God I conceive to be a perfect blank, just as you find my text is.

"You believe in a church without prophets, apostles, evangelists, etc. Such a church would be a perfect blank, as compared with the church of Christ, and this agrees with my text.

"You have located your heaven beyond the bounds of time and space. It exists nowhere, and consequently your heaven is blank, like unto my text."

The missionary continued, systematically critiquing many tenets of the faith of his hearers. He proclaimed many principles of the restored gospel, and ended his discourse by asking, "Have I stuck to the text and does that satisfy you?"

The missionary then sat down and one of the prominent men present, John B. Floyd, announced, "If you are not a lawyer, you ought to be one." Mr. Floyd then turned to the congregation and asked them to supply funds to buy the missionary a new suit. The people responded warmly, some saying they were good for a 'sleeve' or a 'trouser leg' or a pair of socks till sufficient funds had been collected to furnish the missionary with an outfit more suitable to his talents.

The missionary, Jedediah M. Grant, continued his missionary work throughout his life, serving as an apostle in the Quorum of the Twelve, as a counselor to Brigham Young, and as mayor of Salt Lake City.

A Gospel Lesson

In 1876 a group of missionaries was sent to the Lamanites in the Indian territory of Arizona. Missionary headquarters were set up at an old Indian village known as Moenkopi.

In July the missionaries prepared a great feast to celebrate American Independence Day and Utah Pioneer Day. On the morning of the celebration, Sister Elvira Martineau Johnson saw a cloud of dust many miles out on the desert. The missionaries were gathered from their preparations to meet a band of angry Navajos and accompanying Piutes as they rode up on their horses.

The leader of the Indians, a Navajo called Chief Piecon, addressed Brother James S. Brown as the leader of the missionaries. Chief Piecon said a great wrong had been done. Pushing forward a boy who the chief made known was his son, Piecon explained that the lad had killed three cows belonging to a pioneer settlement called Sunset. Chief Piecon had now come to Brother Brown asking him to be the judge, to pass judgment on the perpetrator of the crime. Chief Piecon said he would accept any judgment for this crime committed against white people, even if it was the punishment of death for the boy.

Brother Brown argued that the crime was not that severe. They should all go to Sunset and talk with the settlers. A price would be fixed for the value of the cattle, restitution made, and all forgiven.

"What of punishment?" the chief persisted. Brother Brown continued to argue that restitution was enough. No one need be hurt.

The missionaries then invited the Indians to join them in their festivities and the Indians sat down to an ample meal.

As the meal progressed the angry Indians relaxed and a more friendly atmosphere prevailed. Then Chief Piecon confessed the truth about the incident. It was not his boy who had killed the cattle. The settlers from Sunset had killed three cattle belonging to the Indians. Chief Piecon had hoped to get Brother Brown to pronounce the judgment so that the chief and his Indians could carry it out on the Sunset settlers. That way the judgment would be fair for both Indian and white.

After the feast, Brother Brown went with the Indians to Sunset where he learned the near-starving settlers had found what they thought were three stray cattle out on the range, and had taken them. The settlers reimbursed the Indians for the value of the cattle with supplies that they did have. The Indians were satisfied. An Indian war was averted, because a missionary remembered the lesson: "Do unto others . . ."

The Explosion and the School

It was spring, 1876, just before April Conference. Karl G. Maeser was teaching in a schoolhouse in Salt Lake City. Suddenly there was a terrific explosion which rocked the schoolhouse and caused plaster to fall from the ceiling. The students were dismissed till the schoolhouse could be repaired and inspected. Brother Maeser then went in search of Bishop Sharp, who was over him in authority. He couldn't find Bishop Sharp. He learned that the explosion occurred on Arsenal Hill (where the State Capitol now stands) . Finally, Brother Maeser was told that Bishop Sharp was in speaking with Brigham Young in the President's office. Brother Maeser entered and reported his actions and the condition of the schoolhouse to Bishop Sharp.

President Young, who had been watching Brother Maeser, broke into the conversation. "Brother Maeser, I have another mission for you," he said.

Brother Maeser was shocked. He was just beginning to regain his finances after his previous mission for the Church. And now President Young wanted him to go on another mission. He was astounded.

"Yes," said President Young. "We have been considering the establishment of a Church school and have been looking around for a man—the man to take charge. You are the man, Brother Maeser. We want you to go to Provo, there to organize and conduct an academy to be established in the name of the Church—a Church school."

Brother Maeser did go to Provo and he began the school that is now today Brigham Young University.

The Little Girl Who Smoked a Pipe

Life on the frontiers of America often made it difficult for children to receive adequate education or training. One little girl smoked a pipe. Her grandmother had smoked a pipe, and from the time the little girl was old enough to hold a pipe in her hands, her grandmother had her light and start her pipe. This gave the little girl a taste for smoking. The little girl smoked her own pipes for several years while growing up. She knew it was wrong to smoke a pipe because she was a Mormon, and had been told so, but she continued. After several years of struggling with her conscience, she gave up her pipe.

The little girl dreamed of someday becoming a teacher. She would get a pile of sticks and set them up, pretending the sticks were students. She would play that she was the teacher. Although this was her dream, her own education was too limited. She never achieved the schooling and credentials to make her an acceptable teacher in the public schools. This was a dream she never reached.

The little girl grew up. As a wife and mother in a Utah settlement, she became troubled by the lack of training for the community children, the same lack she had suffered as a child. She wrote: was always an earnest thinker, and naturally of a religious turn of mind. . . . I had reflected seriously upon the necessity of more strict discipline for our little boys. Many of them were allowed to be out late at night; and certainly some of the larger ones well deserved the undesirable name of 'hoodlum'." She was also concerned for the girls, knowing from personal experience that little girls can get into trouble too.

The young woman had an idea to give training to children. She proposed the idea to Eliza R. Snow and Emmeline B. Wells of Salt Lake City. The women liked the idea and presented it to President John Taylor and the Council of the Twelve. The idea was approved. In 1878, Aurelia Spencer Rogers, the woman who had smoked pipes as a girl, established the first "Primary" of the Church in Farmington, Utah. The Primary organization soon spread throughout the Church.

Aurelia Spencer Rogers died six days after the forty-fourth anniversary of the founding of Primary, leaving a legacy for millions of children after her. Though she had never realized her dream of becoming a public school teacher, in the end, Aurelia became one of the greatest teachers of all.

The Important Book

In 1887 a young man wrote a book. He had no knowledge of the American West and knew nothing about The Church of Jesus Christ of Latter-day Saints. Still, he had heard references to "Mormons" in the lurid English tabloids and decided that what he didn't know he would make up.

According to his "made up" history, the American West, from Nebraska to California, was a huge alkali desert. The Mormons were a group of 10,000 people who, in one huge train of wagons pulled by horses, came to the robbers' roost of Salt Lake City.

The Mormons, according to the author, were worse than the "Inquisition of Seville" or the "secret societies of Italy." No non-members were allowed among the Mormons. If any member so much as whispered a word against any Mormon leader, he disappeared, never to be seen again. He wrote that wagon trains could not make it across the West without the men being massacred by the Mormons and the women kidnapped and sold into harems.

The Mormons, he said, were ruled by an evil "Council of Four," also known as "The Holy Four." Two of these all powerful Mormon rulers were named Elder Stangerson and Elder Drebber. Each of these men had a son: Joseph Stangerson and Enoch Drebber. Joseph was a wicked man who smoked a pipe. Enoch was a drunkard who was never sober after 12 Noon, who wore masonic jewelry, who frequented "liquor shops" and "gin palaces," who made a habit of sexually assaulting women, and who sometimes tried kidnapping young women. Enoch and Joseph were two of the most powerful young men among the Mormons and they desired to marry the same fair maiden, a virtuous young lady named Lucy. But Lucy abhorred both Enoch and Joseph, and she was engaged to marry another. Joseph murdered Lucy's father so that she would be persuaded to marry him. Instead, she was imprisoned by Enoch in his harem where she died in a few days of a broken heart. Lucy's fiance, Jefferson Hope, vowed revenge on Enoch and Joseph, who fled to England to escape him. Alas, Jefferson found them and murdered them both, and so avenged his dead sweetheart.

When the book was published, it became a lurid sensation, but because of its gross inaccuracies and wild misconceptions, it is rarely heard of today. If it were not for the author's later works, the book would have disappeared completely.

Yet, the book, published in 1887 is important for two reasons. First, it launched the writing career of a young man. Second, there was a character in the book who transcended the bad plot, the contorted facts and the bad reasoning. The book created a detective character who solved the murders of Enoch Drebber and Joseph Stangerson.

The book, *A Study in Scarlet,* launched the career of Arthur Conan Doyle and introduced to the world for the first time the detective, Sherlock Holmes.

Dead Men Pay No Fines

The religious, ethnic and national differences of early Utah settlers often created incidents of conflict and interest. An early report in the Park Record stated: "There have been considerable tensions in Park City of late, particularly between the territories of the Cornish saloons and the Irish saloons. Law enforcement officers are busy nightly pulling the rows and investigating general cussedness. It should be reminded that public drunkenness is an offense. Offenders will be tried before Judge John L. Street. If found guilt, the sentence is a $30.00 fine or 30 days in the Summit County Jail in Coalville. Those who choose the latter will be tied to a horse and quickly dispatched to their destination. Residence in the Coalville Jail includes free lectures by Mormon preachers on the evils of alcohol. According to Judge Street, all offenders have thus far opted to pay the fine."

In 1889 a man traveling to Park City, Utah had nearly reached his destination when he came upon a horrible sight. He saw the hind wheels of a wagon, quilts, and supplies scattered at the foot of a ravine. Nearby lay a dead man. The shocked traveler rushed on to Park City and reported what he had seen. The justice of the peace summoned a coroner's jury. Equipping themselves with whiskey and cigars—Park City was a gentile community—they braced themselves for the awful sight.

They found the scene of the accident and the mangled body lying nearby. After discussion and speculation, the coroner's jury concluded that the man had been riding in his wagon when the horses bolted, threw the man and probably ran over him. Having thus determined the cause of death, the jury decided to remove the corpse to Park City where it would be examined and disposed of. Two of the men took hold of the body to lift it when the dead man opened his eyes and said, "Can't you let a feller sleep?"

One of the jurors said, "Aren't you dead?"

"Not by a long sight," said the man.

He did seem to be drunk, however, and since the party needed an excuse to bring him into Park City now, drunkenness would have to do. He was put in jail that evening and Monday morning was tried and found guilty, though the justice was not sure of what. He was then fined—to pay the expenses of his own death inquest.

The man objected, saying that it was bad enough for a man to pay for an inquest when he is dead, but he wasn't dead and the darned fools ought to know he wasn't. He had to pay anyway.

The Man Who Wouldn't Die

When Wil was three years of age, he fell into a caldron of scalding water. He was so badly burned that it was nine months before he was out of danger. When he was five or six, Wil fell on his head from the top of a barn. Shortly afterward he fell down a flight of stairs, breaking his arm. He narrowly missed being gored by a bull. He fell from a porch and broke his other arm.

Still a boy, he got his leg caught between the headlock and fender post of a sawmill carriage. Luckily, only his leg was broken. He was kicked in the abdomen by an ox. A load of hay fell off of a wagon onto the boy. He came away from it a little smothered but otherwise unhurt.

When Wil was eight he was in a run-away wagon that turned over on top of him. He was not injured. He climbed a tree to procure some bark and fell fifteen feet, landing on his back. A cousin, witnessing the accident, ran to Wil's parents to tell them Wil was dead, but when they arrived at the scene, Wil stood to meet them.

At twelve years of age Wil was drowned in the Farmington River. He was somehow revived by a young man named Bacon.

At thirteen Wil became chilled in a blinding snowstorm. He crawled into the hollow of a tree where he fell asleep and became unconscious. A man miraculously found him, revived him again and took him home.

At fourteen years Wil split open his left instep with an ax which almost went through his foot. Though it took nine months to heal, he didn't lose his foot.

At fifteen Wil was bitten in the hand by a mad dog in the last stages of rabies (hydrophobia). The bite did not draw blood and he survived again.

At seventeen Wil was thrown onto boulders by a horse. He sustained a broken leg and dislocated ankles.

He was once cleaning the breast-wheel of a flour mill when it was accidentally turned on. He leapt down twenty feet to save his life, only to be caught by another wheel which rolled him into the icy pond below. He came away unharmed. On the day he was baptized, a horse kicked him in the head, but only his hat was knocked off. A few months later a gun was accidentally fired, missing Wil by inches. Later, another gun was pointed at his breast and snapped accidentally, but the gun misfired.

Wil was caught by runaway horses that dragged him, his head and shoulders upon the ground, for half a mile. He was bruised but not broken. Once, when felling trees, a tree fell in an unanticipated manner, falling on Wil and crushing him. In thirty days he was walking again.

The near-death misses continued with Wil throughout his life. He finally died of natural causes at the age of ninety-one years. He died after he completed what he had to do. He was the fourth president of The Church of Jesus Christ of Latter-day Saints, Wilford Woodruff.

The Monster of Utah's Dixie

The tale of the Dixie monster is still passed on today. It began in Washington, a little town in Utah's Dixie, in the late 1800's. One day some children discovered huge footprints, about three feet long, on the dusty street. They hurriedly told their parents. When the parents investigated, they found the children's report was true. Later, footprints were found in corrals and along the river bed. The citizens began to feel uneasy. Many believed it was some kind of hoax. The local Indians repeated the legend of a giant that once roamed the land, slaughtering, devouring and carrying off children. Some of the more religious settlers believed it might be one of the Three Nephites. Others believed it might be the Gadianton Robbers.

One night, a dance was held at Bishop Robert D. Covington's two-story rock house. Nearly everyone in town attended the dance. Late in the evening, a group of young men went out to the corral. There they discovered the giant footprints which went all around the building. The monster had come while they'd been in there dancing. A group of men followed the footsteps to rocks where they disappeared.

The footprints were most often discovered in the early morning. They appeared in the streets and in the cemetery.

Trying to track the huge monster, a group of men came upon what appeared to be a giant bed of sage and shrubbery, matted down in places as if a giant person had slept there.

A town meeting was held to figure out what to do. Much of the citizenry was spooked. Wives pleaded with their husbands not to go into the hills alone. The more superstitious among them linked the monster with whatever went wrong. If tools were missing, if the milk soured, if the hens wouldn't lay, if mothers miscarried, it was because the monster was about.

Some men were afraid to go into the hills to collect firewood. Young Ithamar Sprague, a large, gangling Scandinavian youth had to take over much of the wood gathering activity, for he dared to do it.

There are different stories as to how the monster was discovered. Some say that Ithamar Sprague was so pleased with the success of his prank, that he'd come to the point that he wanted to share it. He wanted to share how he'd fashioned the huge shoes and where he'd hidden them, share how he had sneaked out of the dance without anyone seeing him, made the footprints around the building, then secretly returned.

Others say the reason he confessed was to impress a girl.

It was said that Sprague had to leave town for a while to keep from facing the wrath of several irate citizens. Others were glad the ridiculous gag had finally been exposed.

After a while, the prank took on heroic dimensions. Ithamar's genius became recognized. The tale was recounted over the Years, providing the locals with a great deal of laughter

The First Man in the Relief Society

The young man had just turned seventeen when he was called to go on a mission. He felt young, inexperienced, and lacking in gospel knowledge. He had never been far from home. One of the first sisters he met in the mission field looked at him and said, "Does your mother know where you are?"

He replied, "Yes, I think this is the first time in my young life that my mother really knows where I am."

When the mission president first saw this missionary and the other new missionary arrivals he said, "Well, boys, you don't look very good, but you are the best the Lord has, and he will have to use you."

The mission where the young man was sent was to the Maori people of New Zealand where he was daunted by the strange customs and a language he couldn't at all understand. His first assignment was to a little place named Judea.

At the first Church meeting he attended in Judea, he was unable to understand a word of what was being said. After the meeting, a sister who could speak English came up to the Young missionary and said, "Do you know what they said in there, and what they did?"

The missionary answered, "I could not understand a word."

"Well," the sister replied, "you were called and sustained as the secretary of the Relief Society of the Judea Branch."

The seventeen-year-old missionary was not about to be part of the Relief Society. He felt the sisters might keep taking advantage of him without his knowledge, unless he could learn the Maori language fast.

With the specter of his Relief Society calling hanging over him the missionary studied the Maori language eleven hours every day and fasted and prayed till, on his twelfth Sunday in the mission field, he delivered his first sermon in the Maori Language.

He became so proficient in the Maori language that at the end of his mission, the First Presidency of the Church requested that he stay in New Zealand long enough to translate the *Doctrine and Covenants* and the *Pearl of Great Price* into the Maori language and to revise and edit the previous translation of the *Book of Mormon.* He was twenty two when he accomplished this major calling.

There would be many other callings for this missionary, Matthew Cowley, who later served as an apostle in the Council of the Twelve. But the success of his first mission was due, at least in part, to his having been called to a position in the Relief Society.

The Lover Man of Salt Lake City

Mrs. Theresa Werner, a long-time resident of Salt Lake City, had a nephew named Guglielmi. Actually, Guglielmi married into the family, but his relationship with Aunt Theresa was close. She was a second mother to him, for his own mother was dead.

Our story takes place in the 1920's when Mrs. Werner's nephew had a problem, if such a dilemma may be called so. Guglielmi was undeniably attractive to women. Women would follow him in the streets, and stare at him in restaurants.

Guglielmi was a professional dancer and performer. The tango was the popular dance of the day, and when Guglielmi would tango across the polished floorboards of the Saltair pavilion at the Great Salt Lake, mobs of women would push toward him, trying to touch him. Some even swooned.

He was asked to judge a local beauty pageant. Critics were at a loss to discover the young man's charisma, After all, he was not classically handsome—he was rather "Spanish" looking, though of course he was not. Most of Salt Lake City seemed to take him to heart however. The *Deseret News* commented on his influence on the local population.

Though blessed with many gifts, Guglielmi was not a happy man. He sought to be loved and accepted in spite of his success, not because of it. With his wife and Aunt Theresa, he made a trip back to his native country and village, thinking his people would accept him now that he had success. Instead, a mob of villagers, accusing him of flaunting his wealth, attacked his automobile and he was lucky to escape with his wife and aunt. The crushing blow of rejection by his own people followed him the rest of his short life.

When Guglielmi's marriage fell apart, Aunt Theresa tried to keep peace in the family. She encouraged Guglielmi and stood by him through his bouts of depression. She was often his companion, and when his marriage finally ended in divorce, she remained a voice of calm and reason in his life.

At the age of 31, Guglielmi's tempestuous, gifted, charismatic life came to a sudden end. He died of peritonitis. In his will, he left nothing to his wife. To Aunt Theresa he left one third of all he owned. While his siblings came from the old country to dispute and wrangle over what was left of the estate, Aunt Theresa asked only for a picture, a painting of him. She wanted something to remember her troubled nephew. This was the man adored by millions, who danced his love in the Saltair Pavilion, but who never felt loved for himself.

Guglielmi's stage name was Rudolph Valentino. Seventy years have passed since his death and still women put flowers on his grave.

The Justice of Price, Utah

In the early decades of the twentieth century, Willard Erastus Christianson, a son of Mormon pioneers, served as deputy sheriff in Price, Utah. He didn't display his gun or resort to force to keep the citizens in line. Still, he had the uncanny ability to inspire peace and cooperation with the law wherever he went.

The citizens of Price were proud of their effective deputy sheriff, and they made Willard justice of the peace. Crowds would show up in his courtroom to watch Willard dispense justice. Often ignoring the letter of the law, Willard would sometimes overlook legal practices, dismiss lawyers, question the parties involved, examine the witnesses himself, and dispense a judgment according to the spirit of the law, as he saw it. This made him wildly popular with the crowds.

For example, on one occasion a peddler was brought into court for selling without a license. Justice Willard learned that the man had a wife and seven children who were without food and living in poverty. The man explained that he didn't have a license because he had no money for one. Justice Willard acquitted the man. When the prosecuting attorney protested, Willard explained that there was a natural law that precluded the law requiring a license, and that was a person's right to eat. The right to eat had been a law a lot longer and would still be a natural law after all the courts were gone.

Even after the normal age of retirement, Willard continued to serve the citizens of Carbon County. In 1937, at the age of seventy-three, Willard was working as a night policeman for the city of Price. One night a vagrant was plaguing the town and Willard was sent to pick him up and bring him in to jail. Willard found the vagrant in an alley and asked the man to come along with him.

The vagrant exclaimed that no officer would take him, and he yanked out an automatic weapon. But before he could fire, Willard whipped out a gun and pulled the trigger. The bullet struck the gun in the vagrant's hand, sending the gun flying. The vagrant fell to the ground, thinking he'd been shot. Willard bent over the surprised and stunned man and helped him realize he wasn't hit—only the gun had been shot from his hand. Thereafter the vagrant got up and went peacefully with Willard to the jail.

At the trial the vagrant was still in shock, saying he didn't know where Willard's gun had come from. It was as if he'd drawn his gun from the thin air before the vagrant could pull the trigger. He'd been outgunned by a seventy-three-year-old man.

Later, the vagrant was heard to complain that people got a $6,000 reward for shooting Dillinger, but all he got was six months in jail for trying to shoot Willard. By then, he'd learned who the policeman really was, information the citizens of Carbon County knew all along.

Willard Erastus Christianson had been one of the deadliest gun-slingers in the old west. A hot-headed youth who was soon in trouble with the law, Willard was called "The Mormon Kid" in his early outlaw career. He led an outlaw band that included Butch Cassidy, who later led his own outlaw gang. Willard and Butch remained loyal friends through his criminal career. It was Willard who gave Cassidy the name—"Butch."

The years changed Willard. He wanted to reform. He served time at the Utah State Penitentiary for murder. When he was released in 1900, the Governor of Utah gave him a pardon for past crimes so that he could start his life anew.

Willard never disappointed the trust of the governor, and continued to serve people to the end of his days. But by then his real name had been long forgotten. People knew him by his alias: Matt Warner, the outlaw and gunslinger turned lawman and judge.

The Russian Farmer and the American Church

An American walked up to a Russian farmer while he was plowing land. The American accompanied the farmer up and down the furrows while they discussed many topics. Finally the topic of religion was brought up.

"I wish you would tell me about your American religion,' said the farmer.

"We have no state church in America," replied the American.

"I know that," said the Russian, "but what about your American religion? . . . Catholicism originated in Rome, the Episcopal Church originated in England, the Lutheran Church in Germany, but the Church to which I refer originated in America, and is commonly known as the Mormon Church. What can you tell me of those teachings of the Mormons?"

The American said, "I know very little concerning them. They have an unsavory reputation, they . . . are very superstitious."

"I am greatly surprised," said the farmer shaking his head, "and disappointed that a man of your great learning and position should be so ignorant on this important subject." The farmer plowing his fields knew to whom he spoke. The American was Dr. Andrew D. White, former president of Cornell University and an ambassador to Russia.

The farmer continued to correct him. "The Mormon people teach the American religion; their principles teach the people not only of Heaven and its attendant glories, but how to live so that their social and economic relations with each other are placed on a sound basis. If the people follow the teachings of this Church, nothing can stop their progress—it will be limitless. There have been great movements started in the past but they have died or been modified before they reached maturity. If Mormonism is able to endure, unmodified, until it reaches the third and fourth generation, it is destined to become the greatest power the world has ever known."

In the farmer's attempt to learn from the American, he had, conversely, been the teacher. But the farmer was a writer as well as a man who grew his own food. The bulk of his writings are concerned with ethics and religion, but his best known-works are *War and Peace* and *Anna Karenina.* The farmer was Count Leo Tolstoy.

The Unconquerable Foe

Early pioneers attempted to live in peace with the other inhabitants of the Utah territory, but the pioneers had no love whatsoever for one particular creature.

Laws were passed against them. A letter to the *Deseret Evening News* in 1886 maintained that anyone harboring them "or encouraging them about his premises may be considered as an accessory in their depredations." A suggestion for dealing with them went as follows: "All you have to do in order to put them to flight, is to fire off one or two cannons and they will leave instanter (sic)."

In Colorado the state militia was called out to do battle with them.

In 1904 the Utah State Legislature passed a bounty law against them.

Poison was tried, but it poisoned the cattle instead. Smoking them out was tried. Elaborate patented traps were tried. Whitewash was thrown on them. Then there was the recurring suggestion that the creatures should be eaten. Recipes in the early *Deseret Evening News* and *The Contributor* magazine included frying them, roasting them "for that nut like flavor," fricasseeing, making them into preserves, adding them to cakes, stewing them into bisques, and souping them. *The Contributor* magazine said, "The Europeans prefer them simply boiled."

In 1933 the town of Nephi brought in an army of 10,000 to deal with them. Of course, the army that Nephi brought in was an army of turkeys. The Nephites had the idea that turkeys might prevail, as had feathered relatives in an earlier skirmish in Utah history.

The battle against them still goes on today. But what do you expect from such unconquerable foes as locusts, crickets and grasshoppers?

The Man Who Could Not Sing

One of his favorite scriptures was Doctrine ~ Covenants 25:12: "For my soul delighteth in the song of the heart; yea, the song of the righteous is a prayer unto me, and it shall be answered with a blessing upon their heads." Yet, to sing "the song of his heart" was something the young man could not do.

When he was ten years of age he joined a singing class, but the professor told him that he could never learn to sing. As he grew, he kept trying. Once he was practicing singing in the Templeton building and the room in which he was practicing was next to that of a dentist. The people in the hall decided that someone was having his teeth extracted. He had his character read by a phrenologist who told him that he could sing, but that he (the phrenologist) would like to be forty miles away while the young man was doing it.

Friends begged him not to sing. They would say things like, "Come in . . . but don't sing," or "That is as impossible as it is for (him) to carry a tune."

The young man once remarked to Brother Horace S. Ensign that he would be willing to spend four or five months of his spare time if he could only learn to sing one special hymn, "O My Father." Brother Ensign told him it would take perseverance, so the young man practiced the song as many as 115 times in one day. Still, he was teased as having "a voice like a picket fence."

On a trip to Arizona he asked his traveling companions if he could sing one hundred hymns. They took it as a joke and said they were delighted. But by the time the man had sung about forty times, his companions said that if he sang the remaining sixty times they would surely have nervous prostration. The man held them to their word and continued to sing.

The man became a husband and father. He still continued to sing hymns a hundred times on some days, until the day came he was confident he could sing "O My Father." He volunteered to sing in a Sunday School conference. The meeting was packed. Stage fright came over him to such an extent that his voice wavered and he was far off pitch. The song was so bad the audience could not hold in its laughter, in spite of the fact that it was a Church meeting. The man was humiliated and greatly saddened by his monstrous failure. When he got home a daughter said to him, "Papa, I had to laugh during your singing to keep from crying—I was so ashamed of you."

In spite of the hurt he suffered from this occasion, the "song of his heart" burned in him and he continued to practice. He had been so tone deaf that when he sat at a piano he would sing one note and strike another and not know the difference. But over the years something began to change. His ear began to detect mistakes. His "musical deafness" was slowly disappearing.

When he was forty-three years of age the man bumped into Professor Charles J. Thomas, the music teacher who had told him as a child that he would never learn to sing. The man took his old teacher to a corner and sang "God

Moves in a Mysterious Way His Wonders to Perform." The teacher was so astonished that he asked the man to join the Temple Choir. He joined the choir and sang with them for many years. Not only did he sing in the choir, but he served as a member of the Quorum of the Twelve for thirty-six years and as President of the Church for more than twenty-six years.

In later years he stood in General Conference and said, "I have, upon more than one occasion . . . verified the truthfulness of the quotation, 'That which we persist in doing becomes easy to do, not that the nature of the thing has changed but that our power to do has increased,' by practicing a song two hours and then singing it in public without a mistake. I consider it one of the greatest accomplishments of my life that I have learned to sing."

And it was just one of the many accomplishments in the life of President Heber J. Grant.

A Prayer Before Kings

He was a sheep farmer from Parowan, Utah. In his early 20's he returned to school to get his 10th-grade education. The coach working with BYU High School saw a talent in the young athlete—he could jump. He could jump high! The coach worked hard to train the raw athlete and to earn enough money to send him to a national competition. The young man went, jumped, and was chosen to represent the United States in international competition.

He had never been out of Utah—he'd never been so far from home. He'd never seen a big city or competed against star athletes till he went to the national competition and now, suddenly, he was sailing for Europe.

He sailed on the ship *Finland,* with his fellow U.S. teammates. he was a raw country boy, an unseasoned competitor, an unsophisticated Mormon who wouldn't drink. He became the source of amusement and the object of teasing from the other athletes.

The year was 1912. The winds of conflict and change were blowing across Europe. Nationalism caused small disputes to become major issues. Ethnic tensions turned the Balkans into a tinder box. Germany had been building up military might since the late 1800's. The British navy responded by developing their own war technology. Various European countries strove for possession of colonies on other continents. Diplomats jockeyed to contract military alliances. Europe was treading toward war.

In the interest of peace, representatives from around the world supported the athletic competition. Among those in the packed stadium were royalty, aristocracy, diplomats and delegates.

In Stockholm 2,547 athletes were representing 28 nations at the international competition. The stadium was packed with 22,000 spectators, among whom were representatives from nations around the world.

In his competition event, the high jump, there were 57 athletes competing, representing 20 different countries. As the afternoon wore on and the temperature hovered close to 90 degrees, the field was narrowed to six finalists, then three finalists, then two finalists. He already had beaten the world record holder, the legendary Jim Thorpe. The only competitor left was a German athlete named Hans Liesche.

When the bar was raised for the final round, he knew he had never jumped that high in his life. Before the stadium filled with people stood the raw country boy, preparing for his final jump. Then he did an amazing thing. Instead of running, he turned away, walked several yards, and then he knelt down.

Prayer is a sacred and intensely private thing—such a gesture in a public place would be open to ridicule and jeers. But the world was different then. The time and place had a special meaning for those who had gathered there.

He felt it was the right thing to do. When he knelt to pray before the masses, the crowd was hushed. There were no jeers, there were no boos, there was no laughter, only quiet.

He prayed to do the best he could. Then he rose, went back to his starting position, and leaped over the bar!

Afterwards, there were tears in the eyes of fellow athletes. The defeated German, Hans Liesche, walked up to him and kissed him on both cheeks. The King of Sweden, King Gustav, descended to the winners' podium where he laid around his neck an olive wreath and a gold medal—the first gold medal ever won by a Latter-day Saint in the Olympics: Alma Richards.

The Mormon and the Gangsters

Sam was a farm boy from Franklin, Idaho. he went to Utah State University, served a mission to the Hawaiian islands, went to law school at George Washington University, then went to work at the U.S. Department of Justice in 1929.

Sam soon rose in the ranks of the F.B.I. to become one of the agency's top agents. Despite long hard work, Sam always took Sunday off so he could attend church and teach Sunday School. he was held in such respect by his superiors and fellow agents that no matter where he was and what case he was working on, it was accepted that on Sunday, Sam would take the day off for worship.

In July, 1934, the F.B.I. gave Sam special orders to capture a certain gangster who had been terrorizing part of the country. Sam went to Chicago and met with director Melvin Purvis of the Chicago bureau. Together they tracked down the vicious gangster. As the gangster was coming out of a movie theater on a hot July night, eleven F.B.I. agents attempted to arrest him, but the gangster drew a 38-caliber pistol. Two of the agents opened fire, knocking the gangster to the ground where Purvis got the gun away from him. The gangster died. The body was taken to the Cook County morgue where the incident was investigated.

Jack Lait, criminologist-author, interviewed the agents. All were happy to be interviewed as part of the team that brought the gangster down. One agent claimed his bullet had brought down the gangster, but when he pulled out his gun, Lait saw it was the wrong caliber. All the agents were glad to pull out and show off their guns, all—except one. Sam didn't want to show off his gun. His gun was only there to do a job, not to show off. He had a long session ahead of him and the inquest took all night. But Sam knew and Lait knew. As Lait said later, "The man who has the deepest notch in his gun in the world is Samuel P. Cowley. He is the man who killed Dillinger."

The head of the F.B.I. sent Sam on his next special job. Another murderous gangster needed to be stopped. In November, Sam and an agent companion spotted the gangster in a fast-moving car with another man and a woman. The agents forced the car from the road in an attempt to arrest him. The gangster opened fire and a gun battle erupted, with bullets whining from both vehicles. The two F.B.I. agents were killed, and their bodies were left lying in a ditch by the road.

The next day the gangster's body was found with nine bullets in it. The fatal shots had come from Cowley's gun.

The funeral services for Samuel Cowley were held in the Assembly Hall on Temple Square in Salt Lake City. Speakers at the funeral included George Albert Smith and John Widstoe of the Council of Twelve, representatives from the F.B.I., the Governor of Utah, a genera!, a senator and many others. Samuel Cowley in death was a hero, for he had helped to bring down two of the deadliest criminals of his time: John Dillinger, and, with his final bullets, "Baby Face" Nelson.

Samuel Cowley was the son of apostle Matthias Cowley and a brother to another apostle, Matthew Cowley. At the funeral Matthew Cowley said that "mortality is but a flash in the pan of immortality; that we pass from this mortal coil into an eternal life which affords greater opportunity for service. . . ." Of Samuel's service Elder Cowley said he did it ". . . for the defense of life, liberty and property; that through the spilling of his blood others may be spared a similar untimely end."

Samuel had died the way he had lived, laying down his life in the service of others.

The Basketball Mission

In 1938, British National basketball was dominated by two teams. On April 18th and 19th the teams squared off to determine the British National Championship. The Championship games were held in London's Wembly Stadium before crowds of thousands. The winning team was then to compete in the first International Basketball Tournament.

Nazism was on the rise in Germany at that time, but the British team, in their Union Jack uniforms, defeated the proud German team 40-35, again in Wembly Stadium.

On Friday, May 6, 1938, the nine members of the British basketball team and their chaperones left Victoria Station, bound for Lille, France and the International finals. The players wore the Union Jack on their lapels as they crossed the channel from Dover to Calais. There was something very odd about this basketball team, however, and passengers all along their journey asked questions about them.

In France, the British basketball team was greeted by ambassadors, dignitaries and all manner of French officials. A crowd of over 5,000 people filled the stadium in Lille, France as teams representing various countries played the International finals. The British team defeated the French team 28-26 to take the International Basketball title. Afterwards, the German and Belgian teams invited the victorious British team to have drinks with them. The British team gladly joined them, drinking lemonade while their hosts had other beverages. And while they celebrated, the British team signed autographs and answered more questions from fans and other players.

The British team manager said of his team: "It was a pleasure to accompany such an exemplary group of young men on this trip as manager. Their conduct at all times was above reproach. On the basketball floor their clean play and sportsmanship made them very popular with the large crowds who saw them play. . . . I am happy to report that they were a distinct credit to the highest traditions of British sportsmanship."

The thing that was so interesting about the British team—the thing that attracted so much curiosity, was that not one of the players was actually British. They were all Americans, though legally residing in Britain. Not only were they all Americans, they were all Mormons. And not only was the British Championship team all Mormons, but the second place British team they had to fight for the national title were all Mormons too. Not only were both teams all Mormons, but they were all Mormon missionaries.

The champion team that took the international title in France—that showed many in the world what Mormon missionaries could do—was made up of: Elder Wilford Kowallis, Elder Bruce Hanks, Elder Parry Sorenson, Elder Edmund Evans, Elder DeLos Rowe, Elder Owen Gladwell, Elder Glen Grimmett, Elder Paul Howells, and Elder Marvin J. Ashton. Elder Marvin J. Ashton went from being an internationally celebrated missionary basketball player to being a member of the Quorum of the Twelve.

The Miracle of the House

World War II was over. Much of London lay in ruins after the constant Nazi bombings from the air. Rubble lay where once there were homes. Blackened shells of buildings stood where once there were shops. Because of the destruction, demand was high for the housing that survived the war. For someone just entering the city, finding a place to stay was an impossibility.

Three men on a mission scoured the city looking for a place to live. The search was discouraging. Major reconstruction was not yet underway. The men continued to search and to pray fervently asking for the Lord's help and trusting it would be granted. Finally, they walked through a narrow alley into a dismal courtyard. Yes, there was a house for rent, at least part of the house. Their prayers were answered. The men had a place to live. Some might call it a miracle.

What was even more miraculous than finding the house, though, was the kind of house they found. It was elegant. The long front hallway seemed as if it could have belonged to a museum. Wrought iron graced and secured the windows. Heavy doors looked as if they belonged in castles. Crafted walnut paneling covered the walls of the rooms. Heavy velvet drapes hung down the windows. Oriental carpets were on the floors. Secret passages led to other parts of the house and there were even hidden storage areas.

It was a miracle that the three men found this house to live in. In a short time they were settled in and working on the next miracle. One of the men was a chaplain, Howard C. Badger of the U.S. Army. Another was a missionary, Frederick W. Babbel who had been called to be an assistant to the third man, Apostle Ezra Taft Benson. Elder Benson had been called to Europe at the closing of World War II to re-establish the missions of the Church in many of the war-torn countries.

It was in this house that Elder Benson commenced the miracle of restoring the Church in Europe.

It is strange sometimes how more than one significant event can occur in one place. There were thousands of houses in London, yet it is odd that more than one inspirational, far-reaching event should come from a single house, with power to impact the world. Elder Benson's work there would influence millions.

Decades before, another man had sat in this house, his house, composing music that would affect millions. For this had been the home of George Frederick Handel. In this house he had written his masterpiece, the *Messiah.*

Eye on Eternities

High on Mount Palomar in California a silver dome sits prominent against the sky. This in the Mount Palomar Observatory. In 1948, the 200-inch, 500-ton Hale telescope was hauled up the mountain and dedicated there. It was the largest observatory in the world. For decades astronomers have used the telescope to gaze on eternities.

Mount Palomar was not always called by that name. There is no written record of what the Indians who lived there called it. Spanish explorers named it Palomar—meaning "pigeon roost." But the Spanish explorers left, and the area was mapped and explored by others who renamed it. For half a century it carried its modern name, until 1901 when nearby citizens petitioned to have the mountain name changed back to the old Spanish name, so, in 1901 it became Mount Palomar once again.

What was the name it was given by California settlers and known by for half a century? Mount Joseph Smith.

The Hidden Talents

World War II in Europe brought unexpected side effects. Church leaders reported that the Saints were never so completely living the commandments: keeping the Word of Wisdom, maintaining church standards, paying their tithes. In Sweden alone, convert baptisms rose, and meeting attendance came up to 85 percent. Tithing increased 300 percent over pre-war figures and fast offerings rose 600 percent over pre-war donations.

The increase of funds also brought problems. One Scandinavian saint, Brother Olaf Sonsteby, was an acting mission president during the war. As the Nazis began occupying regions, they began taking possession of banks and confiscating any denominational funds in those banks. Brother Sonsteby, to outwit the Nazis, constantly moved the Church account from one bank to another bank to another bank, always ahead of Nazi accountants.

Finally, the game became too dangerous. Brother Sonsteby removed all the funds from the banks and buried the Church money in the ground.

After the war, when contact was re-established with Church headquarters, Brother Sonsteby went back to the site where he had buried the hidden treasure. But when he dug it up, there was something wrong with it. Instead of the amount of money he had put in, there was a fortune of 37,000 crowns more money!

Brother Sonsteby was at a loss to explain how all that money got added to the money he had buried. He was also deeply concerned about how to report the unmistakable discrepancy on Church records. The issue was presented to the Church representatives sent to straighten out the records after the war.

Brother Frederick Babbel quipped that this was a single case where buried talents had increased. Brother Sonsteby was relieved when the increase was listed finally as "miscellaneous donations received from an unknown source."

The Guiding Light

It was a night in 1956. Los Angeles was hazed over in smog. A four-engine plane loaded with passengers winged its way toward Los Angeles International Airport. Suddenly, there it was—the beacon of light shining through the night haze. The pilot knew he was on course. As long as he could find the beacon of light, the pilot knew he was on course.

It's today. A 747 jet descends through the nighttime sky over Los Angeles. Just as thousands of pilots before him, the pilot sees the beacon and knows that all is well.

During the energy crunch of the 1970's, the lights of the beacon were once turned out to conserve electricity, but the pilots complained and the lights were restored to the beacon. The beacon stands far above the ground. It is made of aluminum covered in gold leaf reflecting spotlights. It weighs 2,100 pounds and is fifteen and a half feet tall. It's also in the shape of an angel.

The "Angel Moroni"—as he is called—blows an eight foot trumpet eastward as it sits atop the Los Angeles Temple of The Church of Jesus Christ of Latter-day Saints, a visual guide to generations of pilots.

The Actress and the Mariachi Band

A well-known U.S. actress (whose name will not be given) was on a flight to Mexico City. On arrival the passengers began to disembark. When the actress emerged from. the plane, she was greeted by a throng of reporters, officials and news photographers. She was delighted with her admiring crowd. People surged from the terminal in greeting.

A mariachi band even appeared and began to serenade her, though she didn't understand the music they were playing. What the mariachi orchestra was playing was, "We Thank Thee, O God, for a Prophet."

People surged forward and placed sombreros on the heads of two unremarkable, though distinguished-looking gentlemen behind her. The crowd also placed serapes on the two men. The puzzled actress drifted away, unnoticed.

It was September, 1965, and President Hugh B. Brown of the First Presidency and Elder Marion G. Romney of the Council of Twelve were visiting the Mexican saints.

To Remember the Sabbath Day

"Remember the Sabbath day, to keep it holy" (Exodus 20:8). The Church of Jesus Christ of Latter-day Saints has expanded to all corners of the world. The truths of the Gospel are universal. The Sacrament prayer will be the same at a church meeting in Colorado as it is in Japan, although offered in a different language. Many variables of church meetings are different, however. A church meeting may take place in a beautiful chapel in Germany, or a school room in Peru, or a grass-thatched home in the Phillipines, or a small apartment in Turkey, or a bunker on the battle front.

In some countries the culturally designated Sabbath-or 'day of rest'—is on a day other than Sunday—as the Western world observes it. The bread and water of the Sacrament vary from country to country, though the commitment and the Spirit are the same. Some of the meetings are gatherings for hundreds of saints. Other meetings consist of only a few kneeling humbly in prayer. It is important for the saints to remember what is truly essential about worship and keeping the Sabbath day holy.

One of the most unusual Sacrament meetings that ever took place was on Sunday, May 5, 1985. There was trouble getting water for the Sacrament, but miraculously the water problem was solved. Only one man was present for the service, though the prayers of many were with him. He had no access to his scriptures for the Sacrament prayers, but had stored the prayers in his personal scientific reference notebook and he read them from there. For privacy, the man held his Sacrament meeting in his bed, which was much like a Pullman berth. Kneeling to say the Sacrament prayers was a difficulty. He solved this by placing his knees on the ceiling and resting his shoulders against his sleeping bag.

In spite of the fact that this private Sacrament meeting was different than any he had ever worshiped in, the man enjoyed one of the most spiritual Sacrament services of his life. His prayers were being given 190 miles above the earth, surrounded by stars and auroras, with a view of eternities. He renewed his baptismal covenants while traveling weightless at 17,500 miles an hour.

This was the first recorded Sacrament meeting held in outer space. It was held by Don Lind, the first Mormon astronaut and the second Mormon in outer space (behind Jake Garn). It was held on the space shuttle Challenger.

Sources

The Actress and the Mariachi Band

"Actress Finds That Fame is Fleeting." *Church News,* Sept. 25, 1965, p. 11.

Another Mormon Miracle

Smith, Eliza R. Snow. *Biography and Family Record of Lorenzo Snow.* Salt Lake City: Deseret News Company Printers, 1884, pp. 22-23.

The Basketball Mission

"Mormon Missionaries Under the Union Jack." *The Improvement Era,* August 1938, pp. 476, 502-3.

The Chicken That Prophesied

Poulsen, Ezra J., *Joseph C. Rich—Versatile Pioneer.* Salt Lake City: Granite Publishing Co., 1958, p. 201.

Christmas in Nauvoo

Millennial Star (George Q. Cannon, ed.) London: George Q. Cannon, vol. 19, p. 756. Roberts, B. H., *History of the Church.* Vol. 6, pp. 130-40.

The City of Wealth

McPhee, William M. *The Trail of the Leprechaun.* Hicksville, NY: Exposition Press, 1977.

The Disappearing Act of Brigham Young

Salt Lake City: George Q. Cannon & Sons Co., Publishers, 1893. pp. 50-52. Roberts, B. H., *History of the Church.* Vol. 7, pp. 549-51.

Dead Men Pay No Fines

Wasatch Wave, Heber City, Utah, October 12, 1889, pp. 54-55. (As cited in Cheney, Thomas E., ed. *Lore of Faith and Folly,* Salt Lake City: University of Utah Press, 1971.) *Park Record* as cited in Oviatt, Joan and Carter, Dan, *Can't Stand Still.* Salt Lake City: privately published, 1980.

The Explosion and the School

Recollections of Reinhard Maeser about his father, LDS Church Historian's Library.

Eye on Eternities

Heslop, J. M., "Family Lives in Shadow of Giant Eye," *Church News.* January 13, 1973, p. 5. Patton, Annaleone D. *California Mormons.* Salt Lake City: Deseret Book, 1961, p. 146.

The First Man in the Relief Society.

Cowley, Matthew. *Matthew Cowley Speaks.* Salt Lake City: Deseret Book Co., 1976, pp. 2, 275.

The Gothic Beauty.

Cannon Family Historical Treasury. Salt Lake City: George Cannon Family Association, 1967.

A Gospel Lesson

McClintock, James H. *Mormon Settlement in Arizona.* Phoenix: 1921, pp. 157-158.

The Grave With Nobody In It

Oviatt, Joan. *Episodes of Mormon Mystery.* Salt Lake City: Harps in the Willow, Pub., 1983, pp. 23-38. *Deseret News,* May, 1962. *Deseret News,* May 27, 1893, p. 8.

The Hidden Ammunition

Cannon Family Historical Treasury. Salt Lake City: George Cannon Family Association,1967, pp.287-288.

The Hidden Talents

Babbel, Frederick W. *On Wings of Faith.* Salt Lake City: Bookcraft, Inc. 1972, p. 19.

The Island of Refuge

Horner, Hon. John M. "Voyage of the Ship Brooklyn." *Improvement Era,* 9:794-798. Lund, A. William, *Improvement Era,* 54:708.

The Justice of Price, Utah

Warner, Matt. *The Last of the Bandit Riders.* New York: Bonanza Books, 1940.

The Little Girl Who Smoked a Pipe

Rogers, Aurelia S. *Life Sketches of Orson Spencer and Others, and History of Primary Work.* Salt Lake City; George Q. Cannon & Sons Co., 1898. p. 207.

The Lover Man of Salt Lake City

Shulman, Irving. *Valentino.* New York: Pocket Books, 1968. *Deseret News,* August 24, 1926, p. 2 and June 5, 1923.

The Man Who Could Not Sing

Oviatt, Joan C., "I Have Learned to Sing," *Ensign,* September 1984, p. 40.

The Man Who Wouldn't Die

Cowley, Matthias F. *Wilford Woodruff.* Salt Lake City: Bookcraft, 1964, pp. 512.

The Marvelous Invention

Owen, Barbara. *The Mormon Tabernacle Organ.* Salt Lake City; American Classic Organ Symposium, 1990.

A Meeting in California

Ellingford, Cordelia Smith Reeder, "Christian Mobocracy as Described by One Who Experienced It," from Lundwall, N. B., compiler. *The Fate of the Persecutors of the Prophet Joseph Smith.* Salt Lake City: Bookcraft, 1952, pp. 56-61.

The Missionary Who Would be King

Britsch, R. Lanier. *Unto the Islands of the Sea.* Salt Lake City: Deseret Book Company, 1986.

The Monster of Utah's Dixie

Larson, Andrew Karl, "Ithamar Sprague and His Big Shoes," Cheney, Thomas E., ed. *Lore of Faith and Folly.* Salt Lake City: University of Utah Press, 1971, pp. 31-36. Fife, Austin & Alta. *Saints of Sage & Saddle.* Bloomington, Indiana: Indiana University Press, 1956, pp. 272-273.

The Mormon and the Gangsters

Pickett, Calder M. "G-Man: Saint Who Shot Dillinger," *Salt Lake Tribune,* Nov. 16, 1947. "Verbatim Report of Funeral Services in Honor of Samuel Parkinson Cowley in the L.D.S. Assembly Hall, Salt Lake City, Utah," Church Historian's Office.

The Mormons and the Doomed Wagon Train
Rhoades, Gale R. and Boren, Karry Ross. *Footprints in the Wilderness.* Salt Lake City: Publishers Press, 1971.

Mouth-to-Mouth Resuscitation
Snow, Eliza R. *Biography and Family Record of Lorenzo Snow,* pp. 276-79. (LDS Church Historian's Library.)

The Mule That Saved the Mexican Saints
Smith, Sally, "A Choice Memory." (LDS Church Archives.) Fisher, Margaret M. *Utah and the Civil War.* Salt Lake City: Deseret Book Co., 1929, p. 98.

The Mystery of the Bad Food
Patton, Annaleone D. *California Mormons.* Salt Lake City: Deseret Book Co., 1961. Kane, Thomas L., "Address Before the Historical Society of Philadelphia," (cited in *Memoirs of John R. Young.* LDS Church Historian's Library, pp. 31-36.

Mystery of the Missing Bell
Robertson, Frank C. and Harris, Beth Kay. *Boom Towns of the Great Basin.* Denver: Sage Books, 1962, pp. 138-139.

News Report on the Amazon
Dickens, Charles. *The Uncommercial Traveler and Reprinted Pieces,* pp. 222-32.

The Non-Mormons Who Saved a Handcart Company
Benson, Alma, *A Short Biography of My Mother—Recollections of Kersten Erickson Benson Coming to Utah in the Year 1857.* (Manuscript in possession of Joan Oviatt.) Day, Robert B. *They Made Mormon History.* Salt Lake City: Deseret Book, 1968, pp. 129-30.

On One Day

Mirkin, Stanford M. *What Happened When.* New York: Ives Washburn Inc., 1957.

The Pants Rebellion

West, Ray B. *Kingdom of the Saints.* New York: The Viking Press, 1957.

A Prayer Before Kings

Black, William T. *Mormon Athletes.* Salt Lake City: Deseret Book Co., 1980, p. 610.

A Road By Any Other Name . . .

Spencer, Clarissa Young and Harmer, Mabel. Brigham *Young at Home.* Salt Lake City: Deseret Book Co., 1940, pp. 242-43.

The Russian Farmer and the American Church

Yates, Thomas J., "Count Tolstoi and the American Religion," *Improvement Era,* February 1939, p. 94.

The Senator Who Stood Against the War

Roberts, B. H. *A Comprehensive History of the Church.* Vol. 4, pg. 294-95.

A Sermon About Nothing

Lewis, T. B. *Faith-Promoting Stories,* 2nd book printed 1882. (LDS Church Historians Library.)

The Settlement That Failed

Paher, Stanley W. *Las Vegas—As It Began—As It Grew.* Las Vegas: Nevada Publications, 1971. Hart, John L., "LDS in Las Vegas," *Church News,* March 7, 1991, pp. 8-9, 12.

The State of East California

Patton, Annaleone D., *California Mormons.* Salt Lake City, Deseret Book Co., 1961, pp. 120-32.

The Tale of Two Meals

Cowley, Matthias F. *Wilford Woodruff.* Salt Lake City: Bookcraft, 1964, pp. 49-50. Nevins, Allan. *Fremont, Pathmarker of the West.* New York: Longmans, Green and Co., 1955.

Testimony of Sea Gulls

Roberts, B. H., *A Comprehensive History of the Church, Vol. III*, pp.332-33. Cracroft, Stephen G. Interview in possession of author.

To Protect a Prophet

Smith, Lucy Mack. *History of Joseph Smith by His Mother, Lucy Mack Smith,* 1902, pp. 222-24.

To Remember the Sabbath Day

Lind, Kathleen Maughan. *Don Lind—Mormon Astronaut,* Salt Lake City: Deseret Book,1985. Lind, Don L., "LDS Astronauts Relate Their Stories," *Church News,* May 19, 1985, p. 7.

The Trousers That Shocked Utah

Cannon Family Historical Treasury. Salt Lake City: George Cannon Family Association, 1967. p. 137.

The Unconquerable Foe

Oviatt, Joan, "Pioneer Solution: Locust Entre." *Deseret News Magazine,* Sunday, December 2, 1984, p. 7.

The Woman Who Died and Came Back

Woodruff, Wilford. *Leaves From My Journal*, p. 52. Moody, Raymond A. Jr., M.D. *Life After Life.* New York: Bantam Books, 1975.